D0608246

# THE
# SOUP
# BIBLE

Publications International, Ltd.

**Copyright © 2010 Publications International, Ltd.**
All rights reserved. This publication may not be reproduced or quoted in whole or in part by any means whatsoever without written permission from:

Louis Weber, CEO
Publications International, Ltd.
8140 Lehigh Avenue
Morton Grove, IL 60053

Permission is never granted for commercial purposes.

All recipes and photographs that contain specific brand names are copyrighted by those companies and/or associations, unless otherwise specified. All photographs *except* those on pages 7, 17, 31, 71, 103, 113, 119, 121, 133, 147, 161 and 179 copyright © Publications International, Ltd.

Campbell's®, Prego® and Swanson® registered trademarks of CSC Brands LP. All rights reserved.

Pepperidge Farm® registered trademark of Pepperidge Farm, Incorporated. All rights reserved.

Some of the products listed in this publication may be in limited distribution.

**Pictured on the front cover:** Italian Skillet Roasted Vegetable Soup *(page 106)*.

**Pictured on the back cover** *(counterclockwise from top):* Creamy Cauliflower Bisque *(page 162),* Classic French Onion Soup *(page 170),* Chicken Tortellini Soup *(page 124)* and Beef Soup with Noodles *(page 140).*

ISBN: 978-1-68022-191-6

Manufactured in China.

8 7 6 5 4 3 2 1

**Microwave Cooking:** Microwave ovens vary in wattage. Use the cooking times as guidelines and check for doneness before adding more time.

**Preparation/Cooking Times:** Preparation times are based on the approximate amount of time required to assemble the recipe before cooking, baking, chilling or serving. These times include preparation steps such as measuring, chopping and mixing. The fact that some preparations and cooking can be done simultaneously is taken into account. Preparation of optional ingredients and serving suggestions is not included.

Publications International, Ltd.

# CONTENTS

# BEEF & PORK

## hearty beefy beer soup

1 tablespoon vegetable oil

¾ pound round steak, cut into ½-inch cubes

1 large onion, chopped

2 medium carrots, sliced

2 stalks celery, diced

5 cups beef broth

1 bottle (12 ounces) stout or dark ale

¾ teaspoon dried oregano

¼ teaspoon salt

⅛ teaspoon black pepper

1 can (about 15 ounces) kidney beans, rinsed and drained

1 small zucchini, cut into ½-inch cubes

4 ounces mushrooms, sliced

1. Heat oil in Dutch oven or large saucepan over medium heat. Add beef, onion, carrots and celery. Cook and stir until meat is no longer pink and carrots and celery are crisp-tender.

2. Stir in broth, stout, oregano, salt and pepper. Bring to a boil over high heat. Reduce heat to low; simmer 45 minutes or until beef is fork-tender.

3. Stir beans, zucchini and mushrooms into soup. Bring to a boil over high heat. Reduce heat to low; simmer 5 minutes or until zucchini is tender.

*Makes 6 servings*

# bacon potato chowder

**4 slices bacon**

**1 large onion, chopped (about 1 cup)**

**4 cans (10¾ ounces each) CAMPBELL'S® Condensed Cream of Potato Soup**

**4 soup cans milk**

**¼ teaspoon ground black pepper**

**2 large russet potatoes, cut into ½-inch pieces (about 3 cups)**

**2 cups shredded Cheddar cheese (8 ounces)**

**½ cup chopped fresh chives**

1. Cook bacon in a 6-quart saucepot over medium-high heat until it's crisp. Remove bacon with a fork and drain on paper towels. Crumble the bacon.

2. Add the onion and cook in the hot drippings until tender.

3. Stir the soup, milk, black pepper and potatoes into the saucepot. Heat to a boil. Reduce the heat to low. Cover and cook for 15 minutes or until the potatoes are tender. Remove from the heat.

4. Add the cheese and stir until the cheese melts. Serve with the chives.

*Makes 8 servings*

Transporting Tip: Transfer the chowder to a slow cooker. Chowder tends to thicken upon standing, so bring along some SWANSON® Vegetable or Chicken Broth to stir in before serving.

Prep Time: **15 minutes** | Cook Time: **30 minutes**

# ground beef, spinach and barley soup

¾ **pound ground beef**

4 **cups water**

1 **can (about 14 ounces) stewed tomatoes**

1½ **cups thinly sliced carrots**

1 **cup chopped onion**

½ **cup quick-cooking barley**

1½ **teaspoons beef bouillon granules**

1½ **teaspoons dried thyme**

1 **teaspoon dried oregano**

½ **teaspoon garlic powder**

¼ **teaspoon black pepper**

⅛ **teaspoon salt**

3 **cups torn stemmed spinach**

1. Brown beef in large saucepan over medium-high heat 6 to 8 minutes, stirring to break up meat. Drain fat.

2. Stir in water, tomatoes, carrots, onion, barley, bouillon, thyme, oregano, garlic powder, pepper and salt. Bring to a boil over high heat.

3. Reduce heat to low; cover and simmer 12 to 15 minutes or until barley and vegetables are tender, stirring occasionally. Stir in spinach; cook until spinach starts to wilt.

*Makes 4 servings*

# italian cupboard soup

2 **boneless top loin pork chops, cubed**

2 **(14½-ounce) cans chicken broth**

1 **(15-ounce) can chopped tomatoes, undrained**

1 **(15-ounce) can cannellini or great Northern beans, drained**

2 **tablespoons dried minced onion**

8 **ounces fresh spinach leaves, torn**

In deep saucepan, brown pork in small amount of oil; add chicken broth, tomatoes, beans and onion. Bring to a boil, lower heat and simmer for 15 minutes; stir in spinach and cook 2 minutes.

Top each serving with grated Parmesan or Romano cheese.

*Makes 4 servings*

Favorite recipe from **National Pork Board**

ground beef, spinach and barley soup

# split pea soup

1 package (16 ounces) dried green or yellow split peas

7 cups water

1 pound smoked pork hocks *or* 4 ounces smoked sausage links, sliced and quartered

2 medium carrots, chopped

1 medium onion, chopped

¾ teaspoon salt

½ teaspoon dried basil

¼ teaspoon dried oregano

¼ teaspoon black pepper

1. Rinse peas thoroughly in colander under cold running water; discard any debris or blemished peas.

2. Combine peas, water, pork, carrots, onion, salt, basil, oregano and pepper in Dutch oven or large saucepan. Bring to a boil over high heat. Reduce heat to low; simmer 1 hour and 15 minutes or until peas are tender, stirring occasionally. Stir frequently near end of cooking to keep soup from scorching.

3. Transfer pork to cutting board; cut into bite-size pieces. Place 3 cups soup in blender or food processor; blend until smooth.

4. Return puréed soup and pork to Dutch oven. If soup is too thick, add water until desired consistency is reached. Heat through.

*Makes 6 servings*

Tip: To purée soup, carefully pour the hot mixture into the blender. Cover with the lid, removing the center cap, then cover the hole with a towel. Start blending at low speed and gradually increase to high speed, blending to desired consistency.

# kansas city steak soup

½ **pound ground beef**
3 **cups frozen mixed vegetables**
2 **cups water**
1 **can (about 14 ounces) stewed tomatoes**
1 **cup chopped onion**
1 **cup sliced celery**
1 **beef bouillon cube**
½ **to 1 teaspoon black pepper**
1 **can (about 14 ounces) reduced-sodium beef broth**
½ **cup all-purpose flour**

1. Brown beef in large saucepan over medium-high heat 6 to 8 minutes, stirring to break up meat. Drain fat.

2. Add mixed vegetables, water, tomatoes, onion, celery, bouillon cube and pepper to saucepan; bring to a boil.

3. Stir broth into flour in small bowl until smooth. Stir into soup until blended. Bring to a boil. Reduce heat to low; cover and simmer 15 minutes, stirring frequently.

*Makes 6 servings*

Note: If time permits, let the soup simmer an additional 30 minutes to allow the flavors to blend.

# kielbasa & cabbage soup

1 pound Polish kielbasa, cut into ½-inch cubes
1 package (16 ounces) coleslaw mix (shredded green cabbage and carrots)
3 cans (14½ ounces each) beef broth
1 can (12 ounces) beer or nonalcoholic malt beverage
1 cup water
½ teaspoon caraway seeds
2 cups *French's®* French Fried Onions, divided
   Garnish: fresh dill sprigs (optional)

1. Coat 5-quart pot or Dutch oven with nonstick cooking spray. Cook kielbasa over medium-high heat about 5 minutes or until browned. Add coleslaw mix; sauté until tender.

2. Add broth, beer, water, caraway seeds and **1 cup** French Fried Onions; bring to a boil over medium-high heat. Reduce heat to low. Simmer, uncovered, 10 minutes to blend flavors. Spoon soup into serving bowls; top with remaining onions. Garnish with fresh dill sprigs, if desired.

*Makes 8 servings*

Prep Time: 10 minutes | Cook Time: 20 minutes

# fiesta pork soup

1 pound lean ground pork
1 (14½-ounce) can chicken broth
1 (8-ounce) jar picante sauce
⅛ teaspoon ground cumin
⅛ teaspoon ground pepper
1 (11-ounce) can condensed fiesta nacho cheese soup
1 cup small round tortilla chips
¼ cup sour cream

In medium saucepan, cook and stir pork until browned. Drain. Add chicken broth, picante sauce, cumin and pepper; bring to a boil. Reduce heat; cover and simmer 15 minutes, stirring occasionally. Stir in cheese soup; simmer until heated through. Do not boil. Pour into serving bowls; garnish with tortillas chips and sour cream.

*Makes 5 servings*

Favorite recipe from **National Pork Board**

kielbasa & cabbage soup

# pork pozole

**2 tablespoons vegetable oil**

**1 pound boneless pork loin, diced**

**1 large sweet onion, chopped (about 2 cups)**

**3 cloves garlic, minced**

**8 cups SWANSON® Chicken Broth (Regular, Natural Goodness® or Certified Organic)**

**1 teaspoon ground cumin**

**1 chipotle pepper in adobo sauce, minced**

**1 can (14½ ounces) diced tomatoes, undrained**

**1 can (15 ounces) hominy, rinsed and drained**

**¼ cup chopped fresh cilantro**

1. Heat **1 tablespoon** of the oil in a 6-quart saucepot over medium-high heat. Add the pork and cook until it's well browned, stirring often. Remove the pork from the saucepot with a slotted spoon.

2. Add the remaining oil to the saucepot and reduce the heat to medium. Add the onion and garlic and cook until tender.

3. Stir in the broth, cumin, pepper, tomatoes and hominy. Heat to a boil. Return the pork to the saucepot and reduce the heat to low. Cover and cook for 35 minutes or until the pork is tender. Garnish with the cilantro.

*Makes 6 servings*

Kitchen Tip: Hominy is dried white or yellow corn kernels with the germ and hull removed. When canned, it's ready to eat. Ground hominy is also known as corn grits or simply grits.

Prep Time: 15 minutes | Cook Time: 50 minutes

# beefy broccoli & cheese soup

¼ **pound ground beef**

2 **cups beef broth**

1 **package (10 ounces) frozen chopped broccoli, thawed**

¼ **cup chopped onion**

1 **cup milk**

2 **tablespoons all-purpose flour**

1 **cup (4 ounces) shredded sharp Cheddar cheese**

1½ **teaspoons chopped fresh oregano** *or* ½ **teaspoon dried oregano**

**Salt and black pepper**

**Hot pepper sauce**

1. Brown beef in small nonstick skillet over medium-high heat 6 to 8 minutes, stirring to break up meat. Drain fat.

2. Bring broth to a boil in medium saucepan over high heat. Add broccoli and onion; cook 5 minutes or until broccoli is tender. Stir milk into flour in small bowl until smooth. Stir milk mixture and ground beef into saucepan; cook and stir until thickened and heated through.

3. Add cheese and oregano; stir until cheese is melted. Season with salt, black pepper and hot pepper sauce.

*Makes 4 servings*

# harvest soup

½ pound **BOB EVANS® Special Seasonings Roll Sausage**
1 **large onion, finely chopped**
2½ **cups chicken broth**
2 **cups canned pumpkin**
2 **cups hot milk**
1 **teaspoon lemon juice**
 **Dash ground nutmeg**
 **Dash ground cinnamon**
 **Salt and black pepper to taste**
 **Chopped fresh parsley**

Crumble and cook sausage and onion in large saucepan until sausage is browned. Drain off any drippings. Add broth and bring to a boil. Stir in pumpkin; cover and simmer over low heat 15 to 20 minutes. Add milk, lemon juice, nutmeg, cinnamon, salt and pepper; simmer, uncovered, 5 minutes to blend flavors. Sprinkle with parsley before serving. Refrigerate leftovers.

*Makes 6 to 8 servings*

Tip: Canned pumpkin can be stored in a cool, dry place for up to 1 year. Refrigerate any open canned pumpkin in a tightly covered nonmetal container for up to 5 days.

# veggie beef skillet soup

¾ **pound ground beef**
1 **tablespoon olive oil**
2 **cups coarsely chopped cabbage**
1 **cup chopped green bell pepper**
2 **cups water**
1 **can (about 14 ounces) stewed tomatoes**
1 **cup frozen mixed vegetables**
⅓ **cup ketchup**
1 **tablespoon beef bouillon granules**
2 **teaspoons Worcestershire sauce**
2 **teaspoons balsamic vinegar**
⅛ **teaspoon red pepper flakes**
¼ **cup chopped fresh parsley**

1. Brown beef in large skillet over medium-high heat 6 to 8 minutes, stirring to break up meat. Drain fat. Remove from skillet; set aside.

2. Heat oil in same skillet. Add cabbage and bell pepper; cook and stir 4 minutes or until cabbage is wilted. Add beef, water, tomatoes, mixed vegetables, ketchup, bouillon, Worcestershire sauce, vinegar and red pepper flakes; bring to a boil. Reduce heat; cover and simmer 20 minutes.

3. Remove from heat; let stand 5 minutes. Stir in parsley before serving.

*Makes 4 servings*

# long soup

1½ tablespoons vegetable oil
¼ small head cabbage, shredded
8 ounces boneless lean pork, cut into thin strips
6 cups chicken broth
2 tablespoons soy sauce
½ teaspoon minced fresh ginger
8 green onions, diagonally cut into ½-inch slices
4 ounces uncooked Chinese-style thin egg noodles

1. Heat oil in wok or large skillet over medium-high heat. Add cabbage and pork; cook and stir 5 minutes or until pork is no longer pink in center.

2. Add broth, soy sauce and ginger. Bring to a boil. Reduce heat to low; simmer 10 minutes, stirring occasionally. Stir in green onions.

3. Add noodles; cook 2 to 4 minutes or until noodles are tender.

*Makes 4 servings*

# pork and noodle soup

1 package (1 ounce) dried shiitake mushrooms
4 ounces uncooked thin egg noodles
6 cups chicken broth
2 cloves garlic, minced
½ cup shredded carrots
4 ounces ham or Canadian bacon, cut into short thin strips
1 tablespoon hoisin sauce
⅛ teaspoon black pepper
2 tablespoons minced fresh chives

1. Place mushrooms in small bowl; cover with warm water. Soak 20 minutes to soften. Drain; squeeze out excess water. Discard stems; slice caps.

2. Meanwhile, cook egg noodles according to package directions until tender. Drain and set aside.

3. Combine broth and garlic in large saucepan. Bring to a boil over high heat; reduce heat to low. Add mushrooms, carrots, ham, hoisin sauce and pepper; simmer 15 minutes. Stir in noodles; simmer until heated through. Sprinkle with chives just before serving.

*Makes 6 servings*

long soup

# vegetable beef noodle soup

½ **pound beef for stew, cut into ½-inch pieces**
¾ **cup unpeeled cubed potato (1 medium)**
½ **cup sliced carrot**
 1 **tablespoon balsamic vinegar**
¾ **teaspoon dried thyme**
¼ **teaspoon black pepper**
2½ **cups reduced-sodium beef broth**
 1 **cup water**
¼ **cup chili sauce or ketchup**
 2 **ounces uncooked thin egg noodles**
¾ **cup jarred or canned pearl onions, rinsed and drained**
¼ **cup frozen peas**

1. Spray large saucepan with nonstick cooking spray. Heat over medium-high heat. Add beef; cook and stir 3 minutes or until browned on all sides. Remove from pan.

2. Add potato, carrot, vinegar, thyme and pepper to same saucepan; cook and stir 3 minutes over medium heat. Add broth, water and chili sauce. Bring to a boil over high heat; add beef. Reduce heat to low; cover and simmer 30 minutes or until meat is almost fork-tender.

3. Bring soup to a boil over high heat. Add noodles; cover and cook 7 to 10 minutes or until pasta is tender, stirring occasionally. Add onions and peas; heat 1 minute. Serve immediately.

*Makes 6 servings*

# black bean and bacon soup

**5 strips bacon, sliced**

**1 medium onion, diced**

**2 tablespoons ORTEGA® Fire-Roasted Diced Green Chiles**

**2 cans (15 ounces each) ORTEGA® Black Beans, undrained**

**4 cups chicken broth**

**½ cup ORTEGA® Taco Sauce**

**½ cup sour cream**

**4 ORTEGA® Yellow Corn Taco Shells, crumbled**

**Cook** bacon in large pot over medium heat 5 minutes or until crisp. Add onion and chiles. Cook 5 minutes or until onion begins to brown. Stir in beans, broth and taco sauce. Bring to a boil. Reduce heat to low. Simmer 20 minutes.

**Purée** half of soup in food processor until smooth (or use immersion blender in pot). Return puréed soup to pot and stir to combine. Serve with a dollop of sour cream and crumbled taco shells.

*Makes 6 to 8 servings*

Note: For a less chunky soup, purée the entire batch and cook an additional 15 minutes.

Prep Time: 5 minutes | Start to Finish Time: 30 minutes

Tip: Any unused bacon can be kept in the refrigerator for an additional 7 days. Keep the bacon in an airtight container, or wrap well in plastic wrap.

# CHICKEN & TURKEY

## spaghetti soup

2 tablespoons vegetable oil

½ pound skinless, boneless chicken breast halves, cut into cubes

1 medium onion, chopped (about ½ cup)

1 large carrot, chopped (about ½ cup)

1 stalk celery, finely chopped (about ½ cup)

2 cloves garlic, minced

4 cups SWANSON® Chicken Broth (Regular, Natural Goodness® *or* Certified Organic)

1 can (10¾ ounces) CAMPBELL'S® Condensed Tomato Soup (Regular or Healthy Request®)

1 cup water

3 ounces uncooked spaghetti, broken into 1-inch pieces

2 tablespoons chopped fresh parsley (optional)

1. Heat **1 tablespoon** oil in a 6-quart saucepot over medium-high heat. Add the chicken and cook until it's well browned, stirring often. Remove the chicken from the saucepot.

2. Add the remaining oil to the saucepot and heat over medium heat. Add the onion and cook for 1 minute. Add the carrot and cook for 1 minute. Add the celery and garlic and cook for 1 minute.

3. Stir in the broth, soup and water. Heat to a boil. Stir in the pasta. Cook for 10 minutes or until the pasta is tender. Stir in the chicken and parsley, if desired, and cook until the mixture is hot and bubbling.

*Makes 4 servings*

Prep Time: 15 minutes │ Cook Time: 30 minutes

# turkey vegetable rice soup

1½ **pounds turkey drumsticks (2 small)**
8 **cups cold water**
1 **medium onion, cut into quarters**
2 **tablespoons soy sauce**
¼ **teaspoon black pepper**
1 **bay leaf**
2 **medium carrots, peeled and sliced**
⅓ **cup uncooked rice**
4 **ounces mushrooms**
1 **cup fresh snow peas**
1 **cup coarsely chopped bok choy**

1. Place turkey in Dutch oven or large saucepan. Add water, onion, soy sauce, pepper and bay leaf. Bring to a boil over high heat. Reduce heat to low; simmer, uncovered, 1½ hours or until turkey is tender.

2. Remove turkey from Dutch oven; let broth cool slightly. Skim fat; discard bay leaf.

3. Remove turkey meat from bones; discard skin and bones. Cut turkey into bite-size pieces.

4. Add carrots and rice to broth in Dutch oven. Bring to a boil over high heat. Reduce heat to low; simmer, uncovered, 10 minutes.

5. Meanwhile, wipe mushrooms clean with damp paper towel. Trim stems; cut mushrooms into slices.

6. Add mushrooms and turkey to soup. Bring to a boil over high heat. Reduce heat to low; simmer 5 minutes.

7. Cut snow peas in half crosswise. Stir snow peas and bok choy into soup. Bring to a boil over high heat. Reduce heat to low; simmer 8 minutes or until rice and vegetables are tender.

*Makes 6 servings*

# spicy squash & chicken soup

**1 tablespoon vegetable oil**
**1 small onion, finely chopped**
**1 stalk celery, finely chopped**
**2 cups cubed delicata or butternut squash (about 1 small)**
**2 cups chicken broth**
**1 can (about 14 ounces) diced tomatoes with chiles**
**1 cup chopped cooked chicken**
**½ teaspoon ground ginger**
**¼ teaspoon salt**
**⅛ teaspoon ground cumin**
**⅛ teaspoon black pepper**
**2 teaspoons lime juice**
**Fresh parsley or cilantro sprigs (optional)**

1. Heat oil in large saucepan over medium heat. Add onion and celery; cook and stir 5 minutes or until crisp-tender. Stir in squash, broth, tomatoes, chicken, ginger, salt, cumin and pepper.

2. Cover and cook over low heat 30 minutes or until squash is tender. Stir in lime juice. Garnish with parsley.

*Makes 4 servings*

Tip: Delicata and butternut are two types of winter squash. Delicata is an elongated, creamy yellow squash with green striations. Butternut is a long, light orange squash. Both have hard skins. To use, cut the squash lengthwise, scoop out the seeds, peel and cut into cubes.

# southwest corn and turkey soup

**2 dried ancho chiles\* (each about 4 inches long)** *or* **6 dried New Mexico chiles (each about 6 inches long)**

**2 small zucchini**

**1 medium onion, thinly sliced**

**3 cloves garlic, minced**

**1 teaspoon ground cumin**

**3 cans (about 14 ounces each) reduced-sodium chicken broth**

**1½ to 2 cups (8 to 12 ounces) shredded cooked turkey**

**1 can (about 15 ounces) black beans or chickpeas, rinsed and drained**

**1 package (10 ounces) frozen corn**

**¼ cup cornmeal**

**1 teaspoon dried oregano**

**⅓ cup chopped fresh cilantro**

*\*Ancho chiles can sting and irritate the skin, so wear rubber gloves when handling peppers and do not touch your eyes.*

1. Cut stems from chiles; shake out seeds. Place chiles in medium bowl; cover with boiling water. Let stand 20 to 40 minutes or until chiles are soft; drain. Cut open lengthwise and lay flat on work surface. Scrape chile pulp from skin with edge of small knife. Finely mince pulp; set aside.

2. Cut zucchini in half lengthwise; cut crosswise into ½-inch slices.

3. Spray large saucepan with nonstick cooking spray; heat over medium heat. Add onion; cover and cook 3 to 4 minutes or until light golden brown, stirring occasionally. Add garlic and cumin; cook and stir about 30 seconds or until fragrant. Add broth, reserved chile pulp, zucchini, turkey, beans, corn, cornmeal and oregano; bring to a boil over high heat. Reduce heat to low; simmer 15 minutes or until zucchini is tender. Stir in cilantro.

*Makes 6 servings*

# green chile chicken soup
# with tortilla dumplings

8 ORTEGA® Taco Shells, broken

½ cup water

⅓ cup milk

2 onions, diced, divided

1 egg

½ teaspoon POLANER® Minced Garlic

1 tablespoon olive oil

4 cups reduced-sodium chicken broth

2 cups shredded cooked chicken

2 tablespoons ORTEGA® Fire-Roasted Diced Green Chiles

¼ cup vegetable oil

**Place** taco shells, water, milk, **1 diced onion**, egg and garlic in blender or food processor. Pulse several times to crush taco shells and blend ingredients. Pour into medium bowl; let stand 10 minutes to thicken.

**Heat** olive oil in saucepan over medium heat. Add remaining diced onion; cook and stir 4 minutes or until translucent. Stir in broth, chicken and chiles. Reduce heat to a simmer.

**Heat** vegetable oil in small skillet over medium heat. Form taco shell mixture into 1-inch balls. Drop into hot oil in batches. Cook dumplings about 3 minutes or until browned. Turn over and continue cooking 3 minutes longer or until browned. Remove dumplings; drain on paper towels. Add dumplings to soup just before serving.

*Makes 4 to 6 servings*

Tip: For an even more authentic Mexican flavor, garnish the soup with fresh chopped cilantro and a squirt of lime juice.

Tip: For ease of preparation, purchase a cooked rotisserie chicken from your supermarket's hot deli case.

Prep Time: 15 minutes │ Start to Finish Time: 30 minutes

# chicken and homemade noodle soup

**¾ cup all-purpose flour**

**2 teaspoons finely chopped fresh thyme *or* ½ teaspoon dried thyme, divided**

**¼ teaspoon salt**

**1 egg yolk, beaten**

**2 cups plus 3 tablespoons cold water, divided**

**1 pound boneless skinless chicken thighs, cut into ½- to ¾-inch pieces**

**5 cups chicken broth**

**1 medium onion, chopped**

**1 medium carrot, thinly sliced**

**¾ cup frozen peas**

**Chopped fresh parsley**

1. For noodles, stir flour, 1 teaspoon thyme and salt in small bowl. Add egg yolk and 3 tablespoons water. Stir until well blended. Shape into small ball. Place dough on lightly floured surface; flatten slightly. Knead 5 minutes or until dough is smooth and elastic, adding more flour to prevent sticking if necessary. Cover with plastic wrap. Let stand 15 minutes.

2. Roll out dough to ⅛-inch thickness or thinner on lightly floured surface. If dough is too elastic, let rest several minutes. Let dough stand about 30 minutes to dry slightly. Cut into ¼-inch-wide strips. Cut strips 1½ to 2 inches long; set aside.

3. Combine chicken and remaining 2 cups water in medium saucepan. Bring to a boil over high heat. Reduce heat to low; cover and simmer 5 minutes or until chicken is cooked through. Drain chicken.

4. Combine broth, onion, carrot and remaining 1 teaspoon thyme in Dutch oven or large saucepan. Bring to a boil over high heat. Add noodles. Reduce heat to low; simmer 8 minutes or until noodles are tender. Stir in chicken and peas; heat through. Sprinkle with parsley.

*Makes 4 servings*

# turkey albondigas soup

½ **cup uncooked brown rice**

Meatballs

**1 pound ground turkey**

**2 tablespoons minced onion**

**2 teaspoons chopped fresh cilantro**

**2 teaspoons milk**

**1 teaspoon hot pepper sauce**

**¼ teaspoon dried oregano**

**¼ teaspoon black pepper**

Broth

**1 tablespoon olive oil**

**¼ cup chopped onion**

**2 cloves garlic, minced**

**5 cups reduced-sodium chicken broth**

**1 tablespoon hot pepper sauce**

**2 teaspoons tomato paste**

**⅛ teaspoon black pepper**

**4 medium carrots, cut into rounds**

**1 medium zucchini, quartered lengthwise and cut crosswise into ½-inch slices**

**1 yellow squash, quartered lengthwise and cut crosswise into ½-inch slices**

Garnish

**Lime wedges**

**Fresh cilantro leaves**

1. Prepare rice according to package directions.

2. Meanwhile, lightly mix meatball ingredients in medium bowl until blended. Shape mixture into 1-inch balls.

3. For broth, heat oil in large saucepan over medium heat. Add onion and garlic; cook and stir until light golden brown. Add broth, hot pepper sauce, tomato paste and pepper. Bring to a boil over high heat. Reduce heat to low.

4. Add meatballs and carrots to broth mixture; simmer 15 minutes. Add zucchini, yellow squash and cooked rice. Simmer 5 to 10 minutes or until vegetables are tender.

5. Garnish with lime and cilantro.

*Makes 4 to 6 servings*

# bounty soup

**1 to 2 yellow squash (about ½ pound)**
**2 teaspoons vegetable oil**
**¾ pound boneless skinless chicken breasts, cut into ½-inch pieces**
**2 cups frozen mixed vegetables**
**1 teaspoon dried parsley flakes**
**⅛ teaspoon salt**
**⅛ teaspoon dried rosemary**
**⅛ teaspoon dried thyme**
**⅛ teaspoon black pepper**
**1 can (about 14 ounces) reduced-sodium chicken broth**
**1 can (about 14 ounces) stewed tomatoes**

1. Cut wide part of squash in half lengthwise; lay flat and cut crosswise into ¼-inch-thick slices. Cut narrow part of squash into ¼-inch-thick slices.

2. Heat oil in large saucepan over medium-high heat. Add chicken; cook and stir 2 minutes. Stir in squash, mixed vegetables, parsley, salt, rosemary, thyme and pepper. Add broth and tomatoes, breaking large tomatoes apart. Bring to a boil. Reduce heat to low; cover and cook 5 minutes or until vegetables are tender and chicken is cooked through.

*Makes 4 servings*

Prep and Cook Time: 30 minutes

Tip: Yellow squash are also known as summer squash. They have thin, edible skins with a creamy white flesh. Because they are perishable, they should be stored in the refrigerator and used within 5 days of purchase.

# turkey taco soup

- 1 tablespoon olive oil
- ½ cup diced onions
- 1 tablespoon POLANER® Minced Garlic
- 1 pound ground turkey
- 1 tablespoon ORTEGA® Chili Seasoning Mix
- ½ teaspoon salt
- ½ teaspoon black pepper
- 3 cups chicken broth
- 1 can (16 ounces) ORTEGA® Refried Beans
- 1 tablespoon ORTEGA® Fire-Roasted Diced Green Chiles
- 1 cup shredded lettuce
- ½ cup chopped tomato
- 4 ORTEGA® Yellow Corn Taco Shells, crumbled

**Heat** oil in large saucepan over medium heat. Add onions and garlic; cook and stir 5 minutes. Stir in turkey, seasoning mix, salt and pepper. Cook and stir 5 minutes to break up turkey.

**Add** broth, beans and chiles; stir until beans are mixed in well. Cook over medium heat 10 minutes.

**Divide** soup among 6 bowls. Divide lettuce among bowls, and stir in to wilt lettuce slightly. Top each serving with chopped tomato and crumbled taco pieces.

*Makes 6 servings*

Tip: For additional flavor variations, use lean ground beef or ground chicken in this soup.

Prep Time: 5 minutes | Start to Finish Time: 30 minutes

# chicken curry soup

**6 ounces boneless skinless chicken breasts, cut into ½-inch pieces**
**3½ teaspoons curry powder, divided**
**1 teaspoon olive oil**
**¾ cup chopped apple**
**½ cup sliced carrot**
**⅓ cup sliced celery**
**¼ teaspoon ground cloves**
**2 cans (about 14 ounces each) reduced-sodium chicken broth**
**½ cup orange juice**
**4 ounces uncooked rotini pasta**
**Plain yogurt (optional)**

1. Coat chicken with 3 teaspoons curry powder. Heat oil in large saucepan over medium heat. Add chicken; cook and stir 3 minutes or until cooked through. Remove from pan; keep warm.

2. Add apple, carrot, celery, remaining ½ teaspoon curry powder and cloves to same saucepan; cook 5 minutes, stirring occasionally. Add broth and orange juice; bring to a boil over high heat.

3. Reduce heat to low. Add pasta; cover and cook 8 to 10 minutes or until pasta is tender, stirring occasionally. Stir in chicken. Top each serving with dollop of yogurt, if desired.

*Makes 4 servings*

# skillet chicken soup

¾ **pound boneless skinless chicken breasts or thighs, cut into ¾-inch pieces**
 1 **teaspoon paprika**
½ **teaspoon salt**
¼ **teaspoon black pepper**
 2 **teaspoons vegetable oil**
 1 **large onion, chopped**
 1 **red bell pepper, cut into ½-inch pieces**
 3 **cloves garlic, minced**
 3 **cups reduced-sodium chicken broth**
 1 **can (about 19 ounces) cannellini beans or small white beans, rinsed and drained**
 3 **cups sliced savoy or napa cabbage**
½ **cup herb-flavored croutons, slightly crushed**

1. Toss chicken with paprika, salt and black pepper in medium bowl until coated.

2. Heat oil in large deep nonstick skillet over medium-high heat. Add chicken, onion, bell pepper and garlic. Cook and stir 5 minutes or until chicken is cooked through.

3. Add broth and beans; bring to a simmer. Cover and simmer 5 minutes. Stir in cabbage; cover and simmer 3 minutes or until cabbage is wilted. Top each serving with crushed croutons.

*Makes 6 servings*

Tip: Savoy cabbage, also called curly cabbage, is round with pale green crinkled leaves. Napa cabbage is also known as Chinese cabbage and is elongated with light green stalks.

# turkey noodle soup

2 (14½-ounce) cans chicken broth

1 cup water

2 tablespoons chopped fresh parsley

¼ teaspoon poultry seasoning

¼ teaspoon black pepper

2 cups cooked, cubed JENNIE-O TURKEY STORE® Oven Ready Homestyle Whole Turkey

1½ cups frozen mixed vegetables, thawed

4 ounces uncooked linguine or fettuccini

In large saucepan over medium-high heat, combine chicken broth, water, parsley, poultry seasoning and black pepper. Bring mixture to a boil. Add turkey, vegetables and pasta. Return to a boil. Reduce heat to low and cook for 8 to 10 minutes or until pasta is tender, stirring occasionally.

*Makes 4 servings*

Prep Time: 15 minutes │ Cook Time: 30 minutes

# potato chicken soup

2½ pounds DOLE® Red Potatoes, peeled, cut into 1-inch cubes

½ pound DOLE® Mini Cut Carrots, halved

4 cups reduced-sodium chicken broth

½ bay leaf

2 teaspoons olive oil

1 small onion, cut into 1-inch cubes

1 teaspoon dried tarragon leaves, crushed

¼ teaspoon dried thyme leaves, crushed

1½ cups cooked diced chicken

1 to 2 tablespoons minced parsley

⅛ teaspoon salt

• Combine potatoes, carrots, chicken broth and bay leaf in large pot. Bring to boil; reduce heat and simmer 15 to 20 minutes.

• Heat oil in nonstick skillet. Add onion; cook 6 to 8 minutes or until lightly browned. Add tarragon and thyme; cook 30 seconds.

• Add onion mixture, chicken, parsley and salt to soup in pot. Cook 5 minutes longer or until heated through. Remove bay leaf before serving.

*Makes 4 servings*

turkey noodle soup

# chicken soup au pistou

½ **pound boneless skinless chicken breasts, cut into ½-inch pieces**

1 **large onion, diced**

3 **cans (about 14 ounces each) chicken broth**

1 **can (about 15 ounces) whole tomatoes, undrained**

1 **can (about 15 ounces) Great Northern beans, rinsed and drained**

2 **medium carrots, sliced**

1 **large potato, diced**

¼ **teaspoon salt**

¼ **teaspoon black pepper**

1 **cup fresh or frozen green beans, cut into 1-inch pieces**

¼ **cup prepared pesto**

**Grated Parmesan cheese (optional)**

1. Spray large saucepan with nonstick cooking spray; heat over medium-high heat. Add chicken; cook and stir 5 minutes or until chicken is browned. Add onion; cook and stir 2 minutes.

2. Add broth, tomatoes with juice, Great Northern beans, carrots, potato, salt and pepper. Bring to a boil, stirring to break up tomatoes. Reduce heat to low. Cover and simmer 15 minutes, stirring occasionally. Add green beans; cook 5 minutes or until vegetables are tender.

3. Top each serving with pesto; sprinkle with Parmesan cheese, if desired.

*Makes 8 servings*

# FISH & SHELLFISH

## new england fish chowder

¼ **pound bacon, diced**
1 **cup chopped onion**
½ **cup chopped celery**
2 **cups diced russet potatoes**
2 **tablespoons all-purpose flour**
2 **cups water**
1 **bay leaf**
1 **teaspoon salt**
1 **teaspoon dried dill weed**
½ **teaspoon dried thyme**
½ **teaspoon black pepper**
1 **pound cod, haddock or halibut fillets, skinned, boned and cut into 1-inch pieces**
2 **cups milk or half-and-half**
   **Chopped fresh parsley (optional)**

1. Cook and stir bacon in Dutch oven over medium-high heat until crisp. Remove with slotted spoon; drain on paper towels. Add onion and celery to drippings. Cook and stir until onion is soft. Stir in potatoes; cook 1 minute. Stir in flour; cook 1 minute.

2. Add water, bay leaf, salt, dill, thyme and pepper. Bring to a boil over high heat. Reduce heat to low. Cover and simmer 25 minutes or until potatoes are fork-tender.

3. Add fish; cover and simmer 5 minutes or until fish begins to flake when tested with fork. Discard bay leaf. Add bacon and milk; heat through. *Do not boil.* Garnish with parsley.

*Makes 4 to 6 servings*

# chick-pea and shrimp soup

1 tablespoon olive or vegetable oil

1 cup diced onion

2 cloves garlic, minced

4 cans (10½ ounces each) beef broth

1 can (14.5 ounces) CONTADINA® Recipe Ready Diced Tomatoes with Roasted Garlic, undrained

1 can (15 ounces) chick-peas or garbanzo beans, drained

1 can (6 ounces) CONTADINA® Italian Paste with Italian Seasonings

8 ounces small cooked shrimp

2 tablespoons chopped fresh Italian parsley or 2 teaspoons dried parsley flakes, crushed

½ teaspoon salt

¼ teaspoon ground black pepper

1. Heat oil over medium-high heat in large saucepan. Add onion and garlic; sauté for 1 minute.

2. Stir in broth, undrained tomatoes, chick-peas and tomato paste. Bring to boil.

3. Reduce heat to low; simmer, uncovered, 10 minutes. Add shrimp, parsley, salt and pepper; simmer 3 minutes or until heated through. Stir before serving.

*Makes 8 to 10 servings*

Tip: Shrimp can be purchased in many forms from the grocery store: fresh, frozen, raw, cooked, shell-on or shelled. One pound of small raw shrimp will yield 8 ounces of cooked shrimp.

# scallops & mock seaweed soup

**4 ounces spinach**

**3 carrots, peeled**

**6 cups chicken broth**

**4 green onions, sliced**

**2 tablespoons chopped fresh dill**

**2 teaspoons white wine Worcestershire sauce**

**2 teaspoons lemon juice**

**1 pound bay scallops, rinsed and patted dry**

**Salt and white pepper to taste**

1. To cut spinach into thin strips, make V-shaped cut at stem end. Roll up and cut crosswise into ½-inch-thick slices.

2. To cut carrots decoratively, use citrus stripper or grapefruit spoon to make lengthwise grooves into carrots about ¼ inch apart. Thinly slice crosswise.

3. Bring broth to a simmer in large saucepan; add carrot slices. Bring to a boil. Reduce heat; simmer 5 minutes or until carrots are crisp-tender.

4. Add spinach, green onions, dill, Worcestershire sauce and lemon juice; simmer 2 minutes. Add scallops; simmer just until scallops turn opaque. Season with salt and pepper; serve immediately.

*Makes 6 servings*

# oyster stew

1 quart shucked oysters, with their liquor
8 cups milk
8 tablespoons margarine or butter, cut into pieces
1 teaspoon freshly ground white pepper
½ teaspoon salt
  Paprika
2 tablespoons finely chopped fresh parsley

Heat oysters in their liquor in medium saucepan over high heat until oyster edges begin to curl, about 2 to 3 minutes. Heat milk and margarine together in large saucepan over medium-high heat just to boiling. Add pepper and salt.

Stir in oysters and their liquor. Do not boil or overcook stew or oysters may become tough. Pour stew into tureen. Dust with paprika; sprinkle with parsley.

*Makes 8 servings*

Favorite recipe from **National Fisheries Institute**

# shrimp & corn chowder with sun-dried tomatoes

1 can (10¾ ounces) CAMPBELL'S® Condensed Cream of Potato Soup
1½ cups half-and-half
2 cups whole kernel corn
2 tablespoons sun-dried tomatoes, cut in strips
1 cup small or medium cooked shrimp
2 tablespoons chopped fresh chives
  Ground black or ground red pepper

1. Heat the soup, half-and-half, corn and tomatoes in a 2-quart saucepan over medium heat to a boil. Cover and reduce the heat to low. Cook for 10 minutes.

2. Stir in the shrimp and chives and heat through.

3. Season to taste with black pepper.

*Makes 4 servings*

Kitchen Tip: For a lighter version, substitute skim milk for the half-and-half.

Prep Time: **5 minutes** | Cook Time: **20 minutes**

oyster stew

# mediterranean fish soup

**4 ounces uncooked small penne, pastina or other small pasta**
**¾ cup chopped onion**
**2 cloves garlic, minced**
**1 teaspoon whole fennel seeds**
**1 can (about 14 ounces) stewed tomatoes**
**1 can (about 14 ounces) reduced-sodium chicken broth**
**1 tablespoon minced fresh Italian parsley**
**½ teaspoon black pepper**
**¼ teaspoon ground turmeric**
**8 ounces firm, white-fleshed fish, cut into 1-inch pieces**
**3 ounces small raw shrimp, peeled with tails intact**

1. Cook pasta according to package directions. Drain; set aside.

2. Meanwhile, spray large nonstick saucepan with nonstick cooking spray; heat over medium heat. Add onion, garlic and fennel seeds; cook and stir 3 minutes or until onion is tender.

3. Stir in tomatoes, broth, parsley, pepper and turmeric. Bring to a boil; reduce heat and simmer 10 minutes. Add fish; cook 1 minute. Add shrimp; cook until shrimp are pink and opaque. Divide pasta among 4 bowls; ladle soup over pasta.

*Makes 4 servings*

# cranky crab bisque

**¾ pound lump crabmeat or 2 (6-ounce) cans crabmeat**
**⅓ cup dry sherry**
**1 (11-ounce) can tomato soup, undiluted**
**1 (11-ounce) can green pea soup, undiluted**
**1 teaspoon Original TABASCO® brand Pepper Sauce**
**2 cups milk**

Combine crabmeat and sherry in medium bowl; marinate 15 minutes. Heat soups and TABASCO® Sauce in 3-quart saucepan over low heat. Stir in milk until well blended and mixture is heated through. Just before serving, stir in crabmeat mixture; cook until heated through.

*Makes 6 servings*

mediterranean fish soup

# manhattan clam chowder

¼ **cup chopped bacon**
1 **cup chopped onion**
½ **cup chopped carrots**
½ **cup chopped celery**
2 **cans (14.5 ounces each) CONTADINA® Recipe Ready Diced Tomatoes, undrained**
1 **can (8 ounces) CONTADINA® Tomato Sauce**
1 **bottle (8 ounces) clam juice**
1 **large bay leaf**
½ **teaspoon chopped fresh rosemary**
⅛ **teaspoon black pepper**
2 **cans (6½ ounces each) chopped clams, undrained**

1. Sauté bacon with onion, carrots and celery in large saucepan.

2. Stir in undrained tomatoes with remaining ingredients, except clams. Heat to boiling. Reduce heat; boil gently 15 minutes. Stir in clams and juice.

3. Heat additional 5 minutes. Remove bay leaf before serving.

*Makes 6½ cups*

Microwave Directions: Combine bacon, onion, carrots and celery in 2-quart microwave-safe casserole dish. Microwave on HIGH (100%) power 5 minutes. Stir in remaining ingredients, except clams. Microwave on HIGH (100%) power 5 minutes. Stir in clams and juice. Microwave on HIGH (100%) power 5 minutes. Remove bay leaf before serving.

# savory seafood soup

**2½ cups water or chicken broth**
**1½ cups dry white wine**
**1 onion, chopped**
**½ red bell pepper, chopped**
**½ green bell pepper, chopped**
**1 clove garlic, minced**
**½ pound halibut, cut into 1-inch chunks**
**½ pound sea scallops, cut into halves**
**1 teaspoon dried thyme**
**Juice of ½ lime**
**Dash hot pepper sauce**
**Salt and black pepper**

1. Combine water, wine, onion, bell peppers and garlic in large saucepan; bring to a boil. Reduce heat to low. Cover and simmer 15 minutes or until bell peppers are tender, stirring occasionally.

2. Add fish, scallops and thyme; cook 2 minutes or until fish and scallops are opaque. Stir in lime juice and hot pepper sauce. Season with salt and black pepper; serve immediately.

*Makes 4 servings*

Tip: Halibut is considered a lean fish because it has a low fat content. If halibut is not available, cod, ocean perch or haddock can be substituted. When buying fresh fish, store it tightly wrapped in the refrigerator and plan on using it within 2 days of purchase.

# simply special seafood chowder

1 tablespoon olive or vegetable oil

1 medium bulb fennel, trimmed, cut in half and thinly sliced (about 2 cups)

1 medium onion, chopped (about ½ cup)

1 teaspoon dried thyme leaves, crushed

5 cups water

1¾ cups SWANSON® Vegetable Broth (Regular or Certified Organic)

1 can (10¾ ounces) CAMPBELL'S® Condensed Tomato Soup (Regular or Healthy Request®)

1 package (10 ounces) frozen baby whole carrots, thawed (about 1½ cups)

½ pound fresh or thawed frozen firm white fish fillets (cod, haddock or halibut), cut into 2-inch pieces

½ pound fresh large shrimp, shelled and deveined

¾ pound mussels (about 12), well scrubbed

Freshly ground black pepper

1. Heat the oil in a 4-quart saucepot over medium heat. Add the fennel, onion and thyme and cook until the vegetables are tender. Stir in the water, broth, soup and carrots and heat to a boil.

2. Stir in the fish. Cook for 2 minutes. Stir in the shrimp and mussels. Cover and reduce the heat to low. Cook for 3 minutes or until the fish flakes easily when tested with a fork, the shrimp turn pink and the mussels open. Discard any mussels that do not open.

3. Serve the soup with black pepper.

*Makes 6 servings*

Prep Time: 10 minutes | Cook Time: 20 minutes

# tortilla soup with grouper

1 tablespoon vegetable oil
1 onion, chopped
2 cloves garlic, minced
3½ cups chicken broth
1½ cups tomato juice
1 cup chopped tomatoes
1 can (4 ounces) diced green chiles, drained
2 teaspoons Worcestershire sauce
1 teaspoon ground cumin
1 teaspoon chili powder
1 teaspoon salt
⅛ teaspoon black pepper
3 corn tortillas, cut into 1-inch strips
1 cup corn
1 pound grouper fillets, cut into 1-inch cubes

1. Heat oil in large saucepan over medium-high heat. Add onion and garlic; cook and stir until softened. Stir in broth, tomato juice, tomatoes, chiles, Worcestershire sauce, cumin, chili powder, salt and pepper; bring to a boil. Reduce heat to low; cover and simmer 10 minutes.

2. Add tortillas and corn; cover and simmer 8 to 10 minutes.

3. Stir in fish. Simmer, uncovered, until fish begins to flake when tested with fork. Serve immediately.

*Makes 6 servings*

# asian pasta & shrimp soup

**1 package (3½ ounces) fresh shiitake mushrooms**

**2 teaspoons Asian sesame oil**

**2 cans (14½ ounces each) vegetable broth**

**4 ounces angel hair pasta, broken into 2-inch lengths (about 1 cup)**

**½ pound medium shrimp, peeled and deveined**

**4 ounces snow peas, cut into thin strips**

**2 tablespoons *French's*® Honey Dijon Mustard**

**1 tablespoon *Frank's*® *RedHot*® Original Cayenne Pepper Sauce**

**⅛ teaspoon ground ginger**

1. Remove and discard stems from mushrooms. Cut mushrooms into thin strips. Heat oil in large saucepan over medium-high heat. Add mushrooms; stir-fry 3 minutes or just until tender.

2. Add broth and ½ cup water to saucepan. Heat to boiling. Stir in pasta. Cook 2 minutes or just until tender.

3. Add remaining ingredients, stirring frequently. Heat to boiling. Reduce heat to medium-low. Cook 2 minutes or until shrimp turn pink and peas are tender.

*Makes 4 servings*

Prep Time: **10 minutes** | Cook Time: **about 10 minutes**

Tip: To devein shrimp, cut a shallow slit along the back of the shrimp with a paring knife and lift out the vein. This may be easier to do under cold running water.

# tomato-basil crab bisque

  1 tablespoon butter
½ cup chopped onion
  1 can (8 ounces) HUNT'S® Tomato Sauce with Roasted Garlic
  1 cup half-and-half
  1 cup coarsely chopped cooked crabmeat
½ cup chicken broth
¼ teaspoon salt
⅛ teaspoon ground black pepper
¼ cup chopped fresh basil leaves

1. Melt butter in a medium saucepan over medium-high heat. Add onion; cook 3 minutes or until tender, stirring frequently.

2. Add tomato sauce, half-and-half, crab, broth, salt and pepper. Bring just to a boil; reduce heat to low. Cover tightly and simmer 5 minutes. Sprinkle with basil before serving.

*Makes 4 servings*

# west coast bouillabaisse

  1 cup sliced onion
  2 stalks celery, cut diagonally into slices
  2 cloves garlic, minced
  1 tablespoon vegetable oil
  4 cups chicken broth
  1 can (28 ounces) tomatoes with juice, cut up
  1 can (6½ ounces) minced clams with juice
½ cup dry white wine
  1 teaspoon Worcestershire sauce
½ teaspoon dried thyme, crushed
¼ teaspoon bottled hot pepper sauce
  1 bay leaf
  1 cup frozen cooked bay shrimp, thawed
  1 (6.4-ounce) STARKIST Flavor Fresh Pouch® Tuna (Albacore or Chunk Light)
    Salt and pepper to taste
  6 slices lemon
  6 slices French bread

*continued on page 78*

tomato-basil crab bisque

In Dutch oven sauté onion, celery and garlic in oil for 3 minutes. Stir in broth, tomatoes with juice, clams with juice, wine, Worcestershire, thyme, hot pepper sauce and bay leaf. Bring to a boil; reduce heat. Simmer for 15 minutes. Stir in shrimp and tuna; cook for 2 minutes to heat. Remove bay leaf. Season with salt and pepper. Garnish with lemon slices and serve with bread.

*Makes 6 servings*

# cajun shrimp and potato chowder

1 tablespoon olive oil

½ pound medium shrimp (26 to 30 count), peeled, deveined (thawed if frozen)

½ cup chopped onion

½ cup chopped green bell pepper

2 cups SIMPLY POTATOES® Homestyle Slices, chopped slightly

1 can (14 ounces) chicken broth

2 teaspoons Cajun seasoning

2 tablespoons all-purpose flour

2 tablespoons water

1 can (14½ ounces) diced tomatoes, undrained

1. Heat oil in 2-quart saucepan over medium heat. Add shrimp, onion and green pepper. Cook, stirring occasionally, until shrimp is no longer pink. Add **Simply Potatoes®**, broth and Cajun seasoning. Bring to a boil. Reduce heat to low. Cook, stirring occasionally, until **Simply Potatoes®** are tender (20 to 25 minutes).

2. In small bowl, combine flour and water; stir until smooth. Add flour mixture to soup. Stir in tomatoes. Cook until soup is thickened and heated through.

*Makes 4 servings*

Total Time: **35 minutes**

cajun shrimp and potato chowder

# VEGETABLES & BEANS

## curried vegetable rice soup

1 package (16 ounces) frozen stir-fry vegetables
1 can (about 14 ounces) vegetable broth
¾ cup uncooked instant brown rice
2 teaspoons curry powder
½ teaspoon salt
½ teaspoon hot pepper sauce
1 can (14 ounces) unsweetened coconut milk
1 tablespoon lime juice

1. Combine vegetables and broth in large saucepan. Cover and bring to a boil over high heat. Stir in rice, curry powder, salt and hot pepper sauce. Reduce heat to low; cover and simmer 8 minutes or until rice is tender, stirring once.

2. Stir in coconut milk; cook 3 minutes or until heated through. Remove from heat; stir in lime juice.

*Makes 4 servings*

Tip: For a lighter soup with less fat and fewer calories, substitute light unsweetened coconut milk. Most large supermarkets carry this in their international foods section.

Prep and Cook Time: 15 minutes

# white bean and escarole soup

**1½ cups dried baby lima beans**

**1 teaspoon olive oil**

**½ cup chopped celery**

**⅓ cup coarsely chopped onion**

**2 cloves garlic, minced**

**2 cans (about 14 ounces each) whole tomatoes, undrained, chopped**

**½ cup chopped fresh parsley**

**2 tablespoons chopped fresh rosemary**

**¼ teaspoon black pepper**

**3 cups shredded escarole**

1. Place lima beans in large glass bowl; cover completely with water. Soak 6 to 8 hours or overnight. Drain beans; place in large saucepan. Cover beans with about 3 cups water. Bring to a boil over high heat. Reduce heat to low; cover and simmer about 1 hour or until soft. Drain; return to saucepan and keep warm.

2. Heat oil in small skillet over medium heat. Add celery, onion and garlic; cook and stir 5 minutes or until onion is tender.

3. Add celery mixture and tomatoes with juice to beans. Stir in parsley, rosemary and pepper. Cover and simmer over low heat 15 minutes. Add escarole; simmer 5 minutes.

*Makes 6 servings*

Tip: Store dried lima beans (also known as butter beans) in an airtight container in a cool, dry place for up to 1 year. When soaking, do not allow beans to soak for longer than 12 hours or they may start to ferment.

# roasted red pepper salsa soup

2 tablespoons olive oil

1 onion, diced

½ teaspoon POLANER® Chopped Garlic

3 cups chicken broth

2 jars (12 ounces each) roasted red peppers, drained

1 cup ORTEGA® Original Salsa (Medium)

½ teaspoon salt

¼ cup canola oil

4 ORTEGA® Soft Flour Tortillas, cut into ¼-inch strips

1 teaspoon ORTEGA® Chili Seasoning Mix

**Heat** olive oil in large pot over medium heat until hot. Add onion and garlic. Cook and stir 3 minutes. Stir in broth, red peppers and salsa; bring to a boil. Reduce heat to low.

**Purée** soup in blender or food processor in batches until smooth (or use immersion blender in pot). Return puréed soup to pot. Add salt; stir to combine.

**Heat** canola oil in medium skillet over medium-high heat until hot. Drop tortilla strips into oil, several at a time. Carefully turn over when strips begin to brown. Remove from oil and drain on paper towel. Sprinkle strips with seasoning mix. Garnish soup with tortilla strips.

*Makes 6 servings*

Prep Time: 5 minutes | Start to Finish Time: 20 minutes

# ravioli minestrone

1 package (7 ounces) refrigerated 3-cheese ravioli

2 teaspoons olive oil

1 medium onion, chopped

2 carrots, chopped

1 stalk celery, chopped

2 cloves garlic, minced

6 cups water

1 can (about 15 ounces) chickpeas, rinsed and drained

1 can (about 14 ounces) diced tomatoes

3 tablespoons tomato paste

1 teaspoon dried basil

1 teaspoon dried oregano

¾ teaspoon salt

¾ teaspoon black pepper

1 medium zucchini, cut in half lengthwise and sliced (about 2 cups)

1 package (10 ounces) baby spinach

1. Cook ravioli according to package directions. Drain; keep warm.

2. Meanwhile, heat oil in Dutch oven or large saucepan over medium-high heat. Add onion, carrots, celery and garlic; cook and stir about 5 minutes or until vegetables are softened.

3. Stir in water, chickpeas, tomatoes, tomato paste, basil, oregano, salt and pepper. Bring to a boil; reduce heat and simmer 15 minutes or until vegetables are tender. Add zucchini; cook 5 minutes. Stir in spinach; cook 2 minutes or until spinach wilts. Stir in ravioli.

*Makes 8 servings*

Prep Time: 20 minutes │ Cook Time: 27 minutes

# cuban-style black bean soup

**2 teaspoons olive oil**

**1 small onion, chopped**

**1 cup thinly sliced carrots**

**2 jalapeño peppers,\* seeded and minced**

**2 cloves garlic, minced**

**1 can (about 15 ounces) no-salt-added black beans, undrained**

**1 can (about 14 ounces) vegetable or chicken broth**

**¼ cup chopped fresh cilantro**

**¼ cup sour cream (optional)**

**4 lime wedges (optional)**

*\*Jalapeño peppers can sting and irritate the skin, so wear rubber gloves when handling peppers and do not touch your eyes.*

1. Heat oil in large saucepan over medium heat. Add onion, carrots, jalapeños and garlic; cook and stir 5 minutes.

2. Add beans and broth; bring to a boil. Reduce heat to low; cover and simmer 15 to 20 minutes or until vegetables are very tender.

3. Sprinkle each serving with cilantro. Serve with sour cream and lime wedges, if desired.

*Makes 4 servings*

Note: For a smooth, creamy soup, purée soup in batches in a food processor or blender.

# butternut squash soup

**2 teaspoons olive oil**
**1 large sweet onion, chopped**
**1 medium red bell pepper, chopped**
**2 packages (12 ounces each) frozen butternut squash, thawed**
**1 can (10¾ ounces) condensed reduced-sodium chicken broth, undiluted**
**¼ teaspoon ground nutmeg**
**⅛ teaspoon white pepper**
**½ cup half-and-half**

1. Heat oil in large saucepan over medium-high heat. Add onion and bell pepper; cook and stir 5 minutes. Add squash, broth, nutmeg and white pepper; bring to a boil over high heat. Reduce heat; cover and simmer 15 minutes or until vegetables are very tender. Purée soup in saucepan with hand-held immersion blender. Or transfer soup in batches to food processor or blender; process until smooth. Return soup to saucepan.

2. Stir in half-and-half; heat through. Swirl in additional half-and-half, if desired.

*Makes 4 servings*

# santa fe tomato chowder

**1 tablespoon butter or margarine**
**2 teaspoons minced garlic**
**4 ripe tomatoes, chopped**
**1 can (15 ounces) tomato sauce**
**1 cup frozen corn kernels**
**¼ cup chopped fresh cilantro**
**1 tablespoon *Frank's® RedHot®* Original Cayenne Pepper Sauce**
**½ teaspoon chili powder**
**1 ripe avocado, peeled and chopped**
**1 cup (4 ounces) shredded Monterey Jack cheese**
**1⅓ cups *French's®* French Fried Onions**

1. Melt butter in large saucepan; sauté garlic for 1 minute. Add tomatoes and cook 5 minutes. Stir in 1 cup water, tomato sauce, corn, cilantro, ***Frank's RedHot*** Sauce and chili powder.

2. Bring to a boil over high heat. Reduce heat; simmer 10 minutes. Spoon soup into serving bowls; sprinkle with avocado, cheese and French Fried Onions.

*Makes 4 servings*

butternut squash soup

# deep bayou chowder

1 tablespoon olive oil

1½ cups chopped onions

1 large green bell pepper, chopped

1 large carrot, chopped

8 ounces red potatoes, diced

1 cup frozen corn

1 cup water

½ teaspoon dried thyme

2 cups milk

2 tablespoons chopped parsley

1½ teaspoons seafood seasoning

¾ teaspoon salt

Heat oil in large saucepan over medium-high heat. Add onions, bell pepper and carrot; cook and stir 5 minutes. Add potatoes, corn, water and thyme; bring to a boil. Reduce heat; cover and simmer 15 minutes or until potatoes are tender. Stir in milk, parsley, seasoning and salt. Cook 5 minutes.

*Makes 6 servings*

# mushroom barley soup

1 tablespoon olive oil

2 cups chopped onions

1 cup thinly sliced carrots

2 cans (about 14 ounces each) reduced-sodium vegetable broth

12 ounces sliced mushrooms

1 can (10¾ ounces) cream of mushroom soup, undiluted

½ cup uncooked quick-cooking barley

1 teaspoon Worcestershire sauce

½ teaspoon dried thyme

¼ cup finely chopped green onions

¼ teaspoon salt

¼ teaspoon black pepper

Heat oil in large saucepan over medium-high heat. Add onions; cook and stir 8 minutes or until onions just begin to turn golden. Add carrots; cook and stir 2 minutes. Add broth, mushrooms, soup, barley, Worcestershire sauce and thyme; bring to a boil. Reduce heat; cover and simmer 15 minutes, stirring occasionally. Stir in green onions, salt and pepper.

*Makes 4 servings*

deep bayou chowder

# sweet potato bisque

**1 pound sweet potatoes, peeled and cut into 2-inch chunks**
**2 teaspoons butter**
**½ cup finely chopped onion**
**1 teaspoon curry powder**
**½ teaspoon ground coriander**
**¼ teaspoon salt**
**⅔ cup unsweetened apple juice**
**1 cup buttermilk**
**¼ cup water**
    **Fresh snipped chives (optional)**
    **Plain yogurt (optional)**

1. Place potatoes in large saucepan; cover with water. Bring to a boil over high heat. Cook 15 minutes or until potatoes are fork-tender. Drain; cool under cold running water.

2. Meanwhile, melt butter in small saucepan over medium heat. Add onion; cook and stir 2 minutes. Stir in curry powder, coriander and salt; cook and stir about 1 minute or until onion is tender. Remove from heat; stir in apple juice.

3. Combine potatoes, buttermilk and onion mixture in food processor or blender; process until smooth. Pour mixture back into large saucepan; stir in ¼ cup water, if needed, to thin to desired consistency. (If soup is still too thick, add additional 1 to 2 tablespoons water.) Cook and stir over medium heat until heated through. *Do not boil.* Garnish with chives or yogurt.

*Makes 4 servings*

# hearty vegetable pasta soup

1 tablespoon vegetable oil

1 small onion, chopped

3 cups vegetable broth

1 can (about 14 ounces) whole tomatoes, undrained, chopped

1 medium unpeeled potato, cubed

2 carrots, sliced

1 stalk celery, sliced

1 teaspoon dried basil

½ teaspoon salt

⅛ teaspoon black pepper

⅓ cup uncooked tiny bow-tie pasta

2 ounces stemmed spinach, chopped

1. Heat oil in Dutch oven or large saucepan over medium-high heat. Add onion; cook and stir until translucent. Add broth, tomatoes with juice, potato, carrots, celery, basil, salt and pepper; bring to a boil over high heat. Reduce heat to low; simmer 20 minutes or until potato and carrots are very tender and flavors are blended, stirring occasionally.

2. Stir in pasta; simmer 8 minutes or until pasta is tender.

3. Stir in spinach; simmer 2 minutes or until spinach is wilted.

*Makes 6 servings*

# cream of asparagus soup

1 tablespoon margarine or butter

1 small onion, chopped

2 cans (14½ ounces each) chicken broth

1 jar (1 pound) RAGÚ® Cheesy!® Classic Alfredo Sauce

2 packages (10 ounces each) frozen asparagus spears, thawed

1. In 3½-quart saucepan, melt margarine over medium heat and cook onion, stirring occasionally, 5 minutes or until tender. Stir in broth, Ragú Cheesy! Sauce and asparagus. Bring to a boil over medium heat, stirring frequently. Reduce heat to low and simmer 5 minutes or until asparagus is tender.

2. In blender or food processor, purée hot soup mixture until smooth. Return soup to saucepan and heat through. Season, if desired, with salt and ground black pepper.

*Makes 8 servings*

hearty vegetable pasta soup

# chile pepper & corn cream chowder

**2 tablespoons butter**

**1 cup chopped onion**

**2 Anaheim\* or poblano chile peppers, seeded and diced**

**½ cup thinly sliced celery**

**1 package (16 ounces) frozen corn**

**12 ounces unpeeled new red potatoes, diced**

**4 cups whole milk**

**6 ounces cream cheese, cubed**

**1 to 2 teaspoons salt**

**¾ teaspoon black pepper**

*\*Anaheim chiles are mild, long narrow green peppers.*

1. Melt butter in large saucepan over medium-high heat. Add onion, Anaheim peppers and celery; cook and stir 5 minutes or until onion is translucent.

2. Add corn, potatoes and milk. Bring to a boil. Reduce heat to low; cover and simmer 10 minutes or until potatoes are tender.

3. Remove from heat; add cream cheese, salt and black pepper. Stir until cream cheese is melted.

*Makes 4 to 6 servings*

# moroccan lentil & vegetable soup

1 tablespoon olive oil
1 cup chopped onion
4 cloves garlic, minced
½ cup dried lentils, rinsed, sorted and drained
1½ teaspoons ground coriander
1½ teaspoons ground cumin
½ teaspoon ground cinnamon
½ teaspoon black pepper
3¾ cups reduced-sodium vegetable broth
½ cup chopped celery
½ cup chopped sun-dried tomatoes (not packed in oil)
1 yellow squash, chopped
½ cup chopped green bell pepper
1 cup chopped plum tomatoes
½ cup chopped fresh Italian parsley
¼ cup chopped fresh cilantro or basil

1. Heat oil in medium saucepan over medium-high heat. Add onion and garlic; cook and stir 4 minutes or until onion is tender. Stir in lentils, coriander, cumin, cinnamon and black pepper; cook 2 minutes. Add broth, celery and sun-dried tomatoes; bring to a boil. Reduce heat to low; cover and simmer 25 minutes.

2. Stir in squash and bell pepper; cover and cook 10 minutes or until lentils are tender.

3. Top with plum tomatoes, parsley and cilantro just before serving.

*Makes 6 servings*

Tip: Many soups taste even better the next day after the flavors have had time to blend. Cover and refrigerate the soup overnight, reserving the plum tomatoes, parsley and cilantro until ready to serve.

# spring pea & mint soup

1 tablespoon butter

1 tablespoon vegetable oil

3 small leeks, whites only, cleaned and diced (about 2 cups)

4 cups SWANSON® Chicken Broth (Regular, Natural Goodness® or Certified Organic)

1 medium Yukon Gold potato, diced (about 1 cup)

1 package (16 ounces) frozen peas (3 cups)

½ cup heavy cream or crème fraîche

¼ cup thinly sliced fresh mint leaves

1 cup PEPPERIDGE FARM® Croutons, any variety

1. Heat the butter and oil in a 3-quart saucepan over medium heat. Add the leeks and cook until tender.

2. Stir the broth and potato. Heat to a boil. Reduce the heat to low. Cook for 20 minutes or until the potato is tender.

3. Stir in the peas. Cook for 10 minutes or until the peas are tender.

4. Place ⅓ of the soup mixture into an electric blender or food processor container. Cover and blend until smooth. Pour the mixture into a large bowl. Repeat the blending process twice more with the remaining broth mixture. Return all of the puréed mixture to the saucepan. Add the cream and mint. Cook over medium heat until the mixture is hot. Season to taste.

5. Divide the soup among **6** serving bowls. Top **each** serving of soup with croutons.

*Makes 6 servings*

Prep Time: 10 minutes | Cook Time: 45 minutes

# two-cheese potato and cauliflower soup

1 tablespoon butter

1 cup chopped onion

2 cloves garlic, minced

5 cups whole milk

1 pound Yukon Gold potatoes, diced

1 pound cauliflower florets

1½ teaspoons salt

⅛ teaspoon ground red pepper

1½ cups (6 ounces) shredded sharp Cheddar cheese

⅓ cup crumbled blue cheese

1. Melt butter in large saucepan over medium-high heat. Add onion; cook and stir 4 minutes or until translucent. Add garlic; cook and stir 15 seconds. Add milk, potatoes, cauliflower, salt and red pepper; bring to a boil. Reduce heat; cover and simmer 15 minutes or until potatoes are tender. Cool slightly.

2. Working in batches, process soup in food processor or blender until smooth. Return to saucepan. Cook and stir over medium heat 2 to 3 minutes or until heated through. Remove from heat; add cheeses. Stir until cheeses are melted.

*Makes 4 to 6 servings*

Tip: One pound of trimmed cauliflower will yield about 1½ cups of florets. You can also substitute 1 pound of frozen cauliflower florets for the fresh florets.

# italian skillet roasted vegetable soup

2 tablespoons olive oil, divided

1 medium yellow, red or orange bell pepper, chopped

1 clove garlic, minced

2 cups water

1 can (about 14 ounces) diced tomatoes

1 medium zucchini, thinly sliced

⅛ teaspoon red pepper flakes

1 can (about 15 ounces) navy beans, rinsed and drained

3 to 4 tablespoons chopped fresh basil

1 tablespoon balsamic vinegar

¾ teaspoon salt

½ teaspoon liquid smoke (optional)

Croutons (optional)

1. Heat 1 tablespoon oil in Dutch oven or large saucepan over medium-high heat. Add bell pepper; cook and stir 4 minutes or until edges are browned. Add garlic; cook and stir 15 seconds. Add water, tomatoes, zucchini and red pepper flakes. Bring to a boil over high heat. Reduce heat; cover and simmer 20 minutes.

2. Add beans, basil, remaining 1 tablespoon oil, vinegar, salt and liquid smoke, if desired. Remove from heat. Let stand, covered, 10 minutes before serving. Serve with croutons, if desired.

*Makes 4 servings*

# QUICK & EASY

## spicy thai coconut soup

2 cups chicken broth

1 can (14 ounces) light coconut milk

1 tablespoon minced fresh ginger

½ to 1 teaspoon red curry paste

3 cups coarsely shredded cooked chicken (about 12 ounces)

1 can (15 ounces) straw mushrooms, drained

1 can (about 8 ounces) baby corn, drained

2 tablespoons lime juice

¼ cup chopped fresh cilantro

1. Combine broth, coconut milk, ginger and curry in large saucepan. Add chicken, mushrooms and corn. Bring to a simmer over medium heat; cook until heated through.

2. Stir in lime juice. Sprinkle with cilantro before serving.

*Makes 4 servings*

Note: Red curry paste can be found in jars in the Asian food section of large grocery stores. Spice levels can vary between brands. Start with ½ teaspoon, then add more as desired.

# quick and zesty vegetable soup

1 pound lean ground beef
½ cup chopped onion
   Salt and pepper
2 cans (14½ ounces each) DEL MONTE® Italian Recipe Stewed Tomatoes
2 cans (14 ounces each) beef broth
1 can (14½ ounces) DEL MONTE® Mixed Vegetables
½ cup uncooked medium egg noodles
½ teaspoon dried oregano

1. Brown meat with onion in large pot. Cook until onion is tender; drain. Season to taste with salt and pepper.

2. Stir in remaining ingredients. Bring to boil; reduce heat.

3. Cover and simmer 15 minutes or until noodles are tender.

*Makes 8 servings*

# new england clam chowder

¼ pound smoked turkey sausage, finely chopped
1½ cups chopped onions
2¾ cups milk
1 medium red potato, diced
1 can (6½ ounces) minced clams, drained, liquid reserved
2 bay leaves
½ teaspoon dried thyme
2 tablespoons butter
¼ teaspoon black pepper
   Saltine crackers

1. Spray Dutch oven or large saucepan with nonstick cooking spray; heat over medium-high heat. Add sausage; cook and stir 2 minutes or until browned. Remove from Dutch oven; keep warm.

2. Spray Dutch oven with cooking spray. Add onions; cook and stir 2 minutes. Add milk, potato, reserved clam liquid, bay leaves and thyme. Cover and simmer 15 minutes or until potato is tender.

3. Remove bay leaves. Stir in sausage, clams, butter and pepper. Simmer until heated through, stirring frequently. Crumble crackers over each serving.

*Makes 4 servings*

quick and zesty vegetable soup

# cheeseburger chowder

1 pound ground beef
1 large onion, chopped (about 1 cup)
2 cans (26 ounces each) CAMPBELL'S® Condensed Cream of Mushroom Soup
     (Regular or 98% Fat Free)
2 soup cans milk
1 cup finely shredded Cheddar cheese (about 4 ounces)
1 cup PEPPERIDGE FARM® Seasoned Croutons

1. Cook the beef and onion in a 3-quart saucepan over medium-high heat until the beef is well browned, stirring often to separate the meat. Pour off any fat.

2. Stir the soup and milk in the saucepan. Cook until the mixture is hot and bubbling. Stir in ½ **cup** cheese. Cook and stir until the cheese is melted.

3. Divide the soup among **8** serving bowls. Top **each** bowl with **1 tablespoon** remaining cheese and **2 tablespoons** croutons.

*Makes 8 servings*

# roasted corn and chicken soup

4 tablespoons olive oil, divided
1 can (15 ounces) yellow corn, drained
1 can (15 ounces) white corn, drained
1 onion, diced
3 tablespoons ORTEGA® Fire-Roasted Diced Green Chiles
½ of 1½- to 2-pound cooked rotisserie chicken, bones removed and meat shredded
1 packet (1.25 ounces) ORTEGA® 40% Less Sodium Taco Seasoning Mix
4 cups chicken broth
4 ORTEGA® Yellow Corn Taco Shells, crumbled

**Heat** 2 tablespoons oil over medium heat in large skillet until hot. Add corn. Cook 8 minutes or until browned; stir often to prevent corn from burning. Add remaining 2 tablespoons oil, onion and chiles. Cook and stir 3 minutes longer.

**Transfer** mixture to large pot. Stir in shredded chicken. Add seasoning mix and toss to combine. Stir in chicken broth and bring to a boil. Reduce heat to low. Simmer 15 minutes. Serve with crumbled taco shells.

*Makes 8 servings*

Tip: To make sure the canned corn is well drained, press excess water out with a paper towel.

cheeseburger chowder

# zesty chicken & vegetable soup

**½ pound boneless skinless chicken breasts, cut into very thin strips**

**1 to 2 tablespoons *Frank's® RedHot®* Original Cayenne Pepper Sauce**

**4 cups chicken broth**

**1 package (16 ounces) frozen stir-fry vegetables**

**1 cup angel hair pasta or fine egg noodles, broken into 2-inch lengths**

**1 green onion, thinly sliced**

1. Combine chicken and ***Frank's RedHot*** Sauce in medium bowl; set aside.

2. Heat broth to boiling in large saucepan over medium-high heat. Add vegetables and pasta; return to boiling. Cook 2 minutes. Stir in chicken mixture and green onion. Cook 1 minute or until chicken is no longer pink.

*Makes 4 to 6 servings*

Prep Time: 5 minutes | Cook Time: about 8 minutes

Tip: For a change of pace, substitute 6 prepared frozen pot stickers for the pasta. Add to the broth in step 2 and boil until tender.

# sausage & zucchini soup

1 pound BOB EVANS® Italian Roll Sausage

1 medium onion, diced

1 (28-ounce) can stewed tomatoes

2 (14-ounce) cans beef broth

2 medium zucchini, diced or sliced (about 2 cups)

2 small carrots, diced

2 stalks celery, diced

4 large mushrooms, sliced

Grated Parmesan cheese for garnish

Crumble and cook sausage and onion in large saucepan over medium heat until sausage is browned. Drain off any drippings. Add remaining ingredients except cheese; simmer, uncovered, over low heat about 40 minutes or until vegetables are tender. Garnish with cheese. Refrigerate leftovers.

*Makes 8 servings*

# new orleans fish soup

1 can (about 15 ounces) cannellini beans, rinsed and drained

1 can (about 14 ounces) reduced-sodium chicken broth

1 yellow squash, halved lengthwise and sliced (1 cup)

1 tablespoon Cajun seasoning

1 pound skinless firm fish fillets, such as grouper, cod or haddock, cut into
    1-inch pieces

2 cans (about 14 ounces each) stewed tomatoes

½ cup sliced green onions

1 teaspoon grated orange peel

1. Combine beans, broth, squash and seasoning in large saucepan. Bring to a boil over high heat. Reduce heat to low.

2. Stir in fish and tomatoes; cover and simmer 3 to 5 minutes or until fish just begins to flake when tested with fork. Stir in green onions and orange peel just before serving.

*Makes 4 servings*

sausage & zucchini soup

# creamy tuscan bean & chicken soup

**2 cans (10¾ ounces each) CAMPBELL'S® Condensed Cream of Celery Soup (Regular or 98% Fat Free)**

**2 cups water**

**1 can (about 15 ounces) white kidney beans (cannellini), rinsed and drained**

**1 can (about 14½ ounces) diced tomatoes, undrained**

**2 cups shredded or diced cooked chicken**

**¼ cup bacon bits**

**3 ounces fresh baby spinach leaves (about 3 cups)**

**Olive oil**

**Grated or shredded Parmesan cheese**

1. Heat the soup, water, beans, tomatoes, chicken and bacon in a 3-quart saucepan over medium-high heat to a boil.

2. Stir in the spinach. Cook for 5 minutes or until the spinach is wilted. Serve the soup with a drizzle of oil and sprinkle with the cheese.

*Makes 4 to 6 servings*

Kitchen Tip: For the shredded chicken, purchase a rotisserie chicken. Remove the skin and bones. You can either shred the chicken with your fingers or use 2 forks.

Prep Time: 10 minutes | Cook Time: 10 minutes

# sensational chicken noodle soup

**4 cups SWANSON® Chicken Broth (Regular, Natural Goodness® or Certified Organic)**
**Generous dash ground black pepper**
**1 medium carrot, sliced (about ½ cup)**
**1 stalk celery, sliced (about ½ cup)**
**½ cup uncooked medium egg noodles**
**1 cup cubed cooked chicken or turkey**

1. Heat the broth, black pepper, carrot and celery in a 2-quart saucepan over medium-high heat to a boil.

2. Stir in the noodles and chicken. Reduce the heat to medium. Cook for 10 minutes or until the noodles are tender but still firm.

*Makes 4 servings*

Prep Time: 5 minutes │ Cook Time: 20 minutes

# quick & easy meatball soup

**1 package (15 to 18 ounces) frozen Italian sausage meatballs without sauce**
**2 cans (about 14 ounces each) Italian-style stewed tomatoes**
**2 cans (about 14 ounces each) beef broth**
**1 can (about 14 ounces) mixed vegetables**
**½ cup uncooked rotini pasta or small macaroni**
**½ teaspoon dried oregano**

1. Thaw meatballs in microwave according to package directions.

2. Combine meatballs, tomatoes, broth, vegetables, pasta and oregano in large saucepan. Bring to a boil. Reduce heat; cover and simmer 15 minutes or until pasta is tender.

*Makes 4 to 6 servings*

sensational chicken noodle soup

# a-b-c minestrone

1 tablespoon olive oil

1 medium onion, chopped

2 medium carrots, chopped

1 small zucchini, chopped

½ teaspoon dried Italian seasoning

4 cups chicken broth

1 jar (1 pound 10 ounces) RAGÚ® Old World Style® Pasta Sauce

1 can (15½ ounces) cannellini or white kidney beans, rinsed and drained

1 cup alphabet pasta

1. In 4-quart saucepan, heat olive oil over medium heat and cook onion, carrots and zucchini, stirring frequently, 5 minutes or until vegetables are tender. Add Italian seasoning and cook, stirring occasionally, 1 minute. Add broth and Pasta Sauce and bring to a boil. Stir in beans and pasta. Cook, stirring occasionally, 10 minutes or until pasta is tender.

2. Serve, if desired, with chopped parsley and grated Parmesan cheese.

*Makes 8 servings*

# chicken corn chowder with cheese

2 tablespoons butter or margarine

⅓ cup chopped celery

⅓ cup chopped red bell pepper

1½ tablespoons all-purpose flour

2 cups milk

1 can (14¾ ounces) cream-style corn

1⅓ cups *French's*® French Fried Onions, divided

1 cup diced cooked chicken

2 tablespoons chopped green chilies

½ cup (2 ounces) shredded Cheddar cheese

1. Melt butter in 3-quart saucepan over medium-high heat. Sauté celery and bell pepper 3 minutes or until crisp-tender. Blend in flour; cook 1 minute, stirring constantly. Gradually stir in milk and corn. Bring to a boil. Reduce heat; simmer 4 minutes or until thickened, stirring frequently.

2. Add ⅔ **cup** French Fried Onions, chicken and chilies. Cook until heated through. Spoon soup into serving bowls; sprinkle with remaining onions and cheese. Splash on *Frank's RedHot* Sauce to taste, if desired.

*Makes 4 servings*

a-b-c minestrone

# chicken tortellini soup

**6 cups chicken broth**

**1 package (9 ounces) refrigerated cheese and spinach tortellini**

**1 package (about 6 ounces) refrigerated fully cooked chicken breast strips, cut into bite-size pieces**

**2 cups baby spinach**

**4 to 6 tablespoons grated Parmesan cheese**

**1 tablespoon chopped fresh chives *or* 2 tablespoons sliced green onion**

1. Bring broth to a boil in large saucepan over high heat; add tortellini. Reduce heat to medium; cook 5 minutes. Stir in chicken and spinach.

2. Reduce heat to low; cook 3 minutes or until chicken is heated through. Sprinkle with Parmesan cheese and chives.

*Makes 4 servings*

# swanson® chicken vegetable soup

**3 cans (14 ounces each) SWANSON® Natural Goodness® Chicken Broth (5¼ cups)**

**½ teaspoon dried thyme leaves, crushed**

**¼ teaspoon garlic powder or 2 cloves garlic, minced**

**2 cups frozen whole kernel corn**

**1 package (about 10 ounces) frozen cut green beans**

**1 cup cut-up canned tomatoes**

**1 stalk celery, chopped**

**2 cups cubed cooked chicken or turkey**

1. Mix broth, thyme, garlic, corn, beans, tomatoes and celery in saucepot. Heat to a boil. Cover and cook over low heat 5 minutes or until vegetables are tender.

2. Add chicken and heat through.

*Makes 6 servings*

Prep Time: 10 minutes │ Cook Time: 15 minutes

chicken tortellini soup

# ravioli soup

1 package (9 ounces) fresh or frozen cheese ravioli or tortellini
¾ pound hot Italian sausage, crumbled
1 can (14½ ounces) DEL MONTE® Italian Recipe Stewed Tomatoes
1 can (14½ ounces) beef broth
1 can (14½ ounces) DEL MONTE® Cut Italian Green Beans, drained
2 green onions, sliced

1. Cook pasta according to package directions; drain.

2. Meanwhile, cook sausage in 5-quart pot over medium-high heat until no longer pink; drain. Add undrained tomatoes, broth and 1¾ cups water; bring to a boil.

3. Reduce heat to low; stir in pasta, beans and green onions. Simmer until heated through. Season with pepper and sprinkle with grated Parmesan cheese, if desired.

*Makes 4 servings*

Prep and Cook Time: 15 minutes

# egg drop soup

2 cans (about 14 ounces each) reduced-sodium chicken or vegetable broth
1 tablespoon reduced-sodium soy sauce
2 teaspoons cornstarch
2 eggs, beaten
¼ cup thinly sliced green onions

1. Bring broth to a boil in large saucepan over high heat. Reduce heat to a simmer.

2. Stir soy sauce into cornstarch in small bowl until smooth; stir into broth. Cook and stir 2 minutes or until soup thickens slightly.

3. Stirring constantly in one direction, slowly pour eggs in thin stream into soup. Sprinkle each serving with green onions.

*Makes 2 to 4 servings*

ravioli soup

# pasta fagioli

**1 jar (1 pound 10 ounces) RAGÚ® Chunky Gardenstyle Pasta Sauce**
**1 can (19 ounces) white kidney beans, rinsed and drained**
**1 box (10 ounces) frozen chopped spinach, thawed**
**8 ounces ditalini pasta, cooked and drained (reserve 2 cups pasta water)**

1. In 6-quart saucepot, combine Pasta Sauce, beans, spinach, pasta and reserved pasta water; heat through.

2. Season, if desired, with salt, ground black pepper and grated Parmesan cheese.

*Makes 4 servings*

Prep Time: 20 minutes │ Cook Time: 10 minutes

# 1–2–3 steak soup

**1 pound boneless beef sirloin steak, cut into 1-inch cubes**
**1 tablespoon vegetable oil**
**½ pound sliced mushrooms (about 2½ cups)**
**2 cups *French's®* French Fried Onions, divided**
**1 package (16 ounces) frozen vegetables for stew (potatoes, carrots, celery and pearl onions)**
**2 cans (14½ ounces each) beef broth**
**1 can (8 ounces) tomato sauce**
**1 tablespoon *French's®* Worcestershire Sauce**
  **Garnish: chopped parsley (optional)**

1. Cook beef in hot oil in large saucepan over medium heat until browned, stirring frequently. Remove beef from pan; set aside.

2. Sauté mushrooms and ½ **cup** French Fried Onions in drippings in same pan over medium heat until golden, stirring occasionally. Stir in vegetables, broth, tomato sauce and Worcestershire. Return beef to pan.

3. Heat to a boil over high heat; reduce heat to low. Cover and simmer 20 minutes or until vegetables are tender, stirring occasionally. Spoon soup into serving bowls; top with remaining onions. Garnish with chopped parsley, if desired.

*Makes 8 servings*

Prep Time: 5 minutes │ Cook Time: 30 minutes

pasta fagioli

# GLOBAL FLAVORS

## black & white mexican bean soup

1 tablespoon vegetable oil

1 cup chopped onion

½ teaspoon POLANER® Minced Garlic

¼ cup all-purpose flour

1 packet (1.25 ounces) ORTEGA® Taco Seasoning Mix

2 cups milk

1 can (about 14 ounces) chicken broth

1 package (16 ounces) frozen corn

1 can (15 ounces) JOAN OF ARC® Great Northern Beans, rinsed, drained

1 can (15 ounces) ORTEGA® Black Beans, rinsed, drained

1 can (4 ounces) ORTEGA® Fire-Roasted Diced Green Chiles

2 tablespoons chopped cilantro

**Heat** oil in large pan or Dutch oven over medium-high heat. Add onion and garlic; cook until onion is tender.

**Stir** in flour and taco seasoning mix; gradually stir in milk until blended. Add remaining ingredients except cilantro.

**Bring** to a boil, stirring constantly. Reduce heat to low; simmer for 15 minutes or until thickened, stirring occasionally.

**Stir** in cilantro.

*Makes 6 servings*

# west african vegetable soup

**2 tablespoons olive oil**

**1 large sweet onion, sliced (about 2 cups)**

**2 cloves garlic, minced**

**4 cups SWANSON® Vegetable or Chicken Broth (Regular or Certified Organic)**

**½ teaspoon ground cinnamon**

**½ teaspoon crushed red pepper**

**2 medium sweet potatoes, peeled, cut in half lengthwise and sliced (2 cups)**

**1 can (14½ ounces) diced tomatoes, undrained**

**½ cup raisins**

**1 bag (6 ounces) spinach, stemmed and coarsely chopped (about 4 cups)**

**1 can (about 16 ounces) chickpeas (garbanzo beans), rinsed and drained**

**Cooked couscous (optional)**

1. Heat the oil in a 6-quart saucepot over medium heat. Add the onion and garlic and cook until tender.

2. Add the broth, cinnamon, red pepper, sweet potatoes, tomatoes and raisins. Heat to a boil. Reduce the heat to low. Cover and cook for 20 minutes or until the potatoes are tender.

3. Add the spinach and chickpeas. Cook until the spinach wilts.

4. Divide soup among **6** serving bowls. Place about ½ **cup** of the couscous on top of **each** bowl of soup, if desired.

*Makes 6 servings*

Prep Time: 15 minutes | Cook Time: 30 minutes

# tofu and snow pea noodle bowl

**5 cups water**

**6 tablespoons chicken-flavored broth powder\***

**4 ounces uncooked vermicelli, broken in thirds**

**½ pound firm tofu, patted dry and cut in ¼-inch cubes**

**1 cup (3 ounces) fresh snow peas**

**1 cup matchstick-size carrot strips**

**½ teaspoon chili garlic sauce**

**½ cup chopped green onions**

**¼ cup chopped fresh cilantro (optional)**

**2 tablespoons lime juice**

**1 tablespoon grated fresh ginger**

**2 teaspoons soy sauce**

*\*Chicken-flavored vegetarian broth powder can be found in natural food stores and some supermarkets.*

1. Bring water to a boil in large saucepan over high heat. Stir in broth powder and vermicelli. Return to a boil. Reduce heat to medium; simmer 6 minutes. Stir in tofu, snow peas, carrots and chili garlic sauce; simmer 2 minutes.

2. Remove from heat; stir in green onions, cilantro, if desired, lime juice, ginger and soy sauce. Serve immediately.

*Makes 4 servings*

Tip: Substitute 5 cups of canned vegetable broth for the water and broth powder.

# japanese noodle soup

1 package (about 8 ounces) Japanese udon noodles
1 teaspoon vegetable oil
1 medium red bell pepper, cut into thin strips
1 medium carrot, diagonally sliced
2 green onions, thinly sliced
2 cans (about 14 ounces each) reduced-sodium vegetable or beef broth
1 cup water
1 teaspoon soy sauce
½ teaspoon grated fresh ginger
½ teaspoon black pepper
2 cups thinly sliced fresh shiitake mushrooms, stems removed
4 ounces daikon (Japanese radish), peeled and cut into thin strips
4 ounces firm tofu, drained and cut into ½-inch cubes

1. Cook noodles according to package directions. Drain; set aside and keep warm.

2. Meanwhile, heat oil in wok or large saucepan over medium-high heat. Add bell pepper, carrot and green onions; cook 3 minutes or until slightly softened. Stir in broth, water, soy sauce, ginger and black pepper; bring to a boil. Add mushrooms, daikon and tofu; reduce heat and simmer 5 minutes.

3. Place noodles in bowls; ladle soup over noodles.

*Makes 6 servings*

# indonesian curried soup

1 can (14 ounces) coconut milk*
1 can (10¾ ounces) condensed tomato soup
¾ cup milk
3 tablespoons *Frank's® RedHot® Original Cayenne Pepper Sauce*
1½ teaspoons curry powder

*You can substitute 1 cup half-and-half for coconut milk BUT increase milk to 1½ cups.*

1. Combine all ingredients in medium saucepan; stir until smooth.

2. Cook over low heat about 5 minutes or until heated through, stirring occasionally.

*Makes 6 servings (4 cups)*

Prep Time: 5 minutes | Cook Time: 5 minutes

japanese noodle soup

# middle eastern lentil soup

1 cup dried lentils

2 tablespoons olive oil

1 small onion, chopped

1 medium red bell pepper, chopped

1 teaspoon whole fennel seeds

½ teaspoon ground cumin

¼ teaspoon ground red pepper

4 cups water

½ teaspoon salt

1 tablespoon lemon juice

½ cup plain yogurt

2 tablespoons chopped fresh parsley

1. Rinse lentils, discarding any debris or blemished lentils; drain and set aside.

2. Heat oil in large saucepan over medium-high heat. Add onion and bell pepper; cook and stir 5 minutes or until tender. Add fennel seeds, cumin and ground red pepper; cook and stir 1 minute.

3. Add water, lentils and salt. Bring to a boil. Reduce heat to low. Cover and simmer 25 to 30 minutes or until lentils are tender. Stir in lemon juice.

4. Top each serving with yogurt; sprinkle with parsley.

*Makes 4 servings*

Tip: Serve with homemade pita chips. Cut 4 pita bread rounds into 6 wedges each. Toss wedges with 1 tablespoon olive oil and 1 teaspoon coarse salt; spread on large baking sheet. Bake at 350°F 15 minutes or until light brown and crisp.

# beef soup with noodles

2 tablespoons soy sauce

1 teaspoon minced fresh ginger

¼ teaspoon red pepper flakes

1 boneless beef top sirloin steak (about ¾ pound)

1 tablespoon peanut or vegetable oil

2 cups sliced fresh mushrooms

2 cans (about 14 ounces each) beef broth

1 cup (3 ounces) fresh snow peas, cut diagonally into 1-inch pieces

1½ cups hot cooked egg noodles (2 ounces uncooked)

1 green onion, cut diagonally into thin slices

1 teaspoon dark sesame oil (optional)

Red bell pepper strips (optional)

1. Combine soy sauce, ginger and red pepper flakes in small bowl. Spread mixture evenly over both sides of steak. Marinate 15 minutes.

2. Heat peanut oil in deep skillet over medium-high heat. Drain steak; reserve marinade (there will only be a small amount of marinade). Add steak to skillet; cook 5 minutes per side for medium-rare or until desired doneness. Let stand on cutting board 10 minutes.

3. Add mushrooms to skillet; cook and stir 2 minutes. Add broth, snow peas and reserved marinade; bring to a boil, scraping up browned bits. Reduce heat to low; stir in noodles.

4. Cut steak lengthwise in half, then crosswise into thin slices. Stir into soup; heat through. Stir in green onion and sesame oil, if desired. Garnish with bell pepper strips.

*Makes 4 to 6 servings*

# brazilian black bean soup

**1 red onion, chopped**

**2 cloves garlic, minced**

**1 can (29 ounces) black beans, drained**

**1 can (14½ ounces) vegetable or chicken broth**

**3 tablespoons *Frank's®  RedHot®* Original Cayenne Pepper Sauce**

**2 tablespoons chopped cilantro**

**2 teaspoons ground cumin**

**2 tablespoons rum or sherry (optional)**

1. Heat **1 tablespoon oil** in 3-quart saucepot. Cook and stir onion and garlic 3 minutes or just until tender. Stir in **1½ cups water** and remaining ingredients *except* rum. Heat to boiling. Reduce heat to medium-low. Cook, partially covered, 20 minutes or until flavors are blended, stirring occasionally.

2. Ladle about half of soup into blender or food processor. Cover securely. Blend on low speed until mixture is smooth. Return to saucepot. Stir in rum. Cook over medium-low heat 3 minutes or until heated through and flavors are blended. Garnish with lime slices, sour cream, minced onion or cilantro, if desired.

*Makes 4 to 6 servings*

Prep Time: 10 minutes │ Cook Time: 30 minutes

Tip: Cilantro is also known as coriander or Chinese parsley.
It is sold in bunches in the produce section of the grocery store.
Cilantro should be stored in the refrigerator in a plastic bag or
in a glass of water. It usually stays fresh for about 1 week.

# wonton soup

¼ **pound ground pork, chicken or turkey**
¼ **cup finely chopped water chestnuts**
2 **tablespoons soy sauce, divided**
1 **egg white, lightly beaten**
1 **teaspoon minced fresh ginger**
12 **wonton wrappers**
6 **cups chicken broth**
1½ **cups stemmed spinach, torn**
1 **cup thinly sliced cooked pork (optional)**
½ **cup diagonally sliced green onions**
1 **tablespoon dark sesame oil**
**Shredded carrot (optional)**

1. For wonton filling, combine ground pork, water chestnuts, 1 tablespoon soy sauce, egg white and ginger in small bowl; mix well.

2. Place 1 wonton wrapper with point toward edge of counter. Mound 1 teaspoon filling near bottom point. Fold bottom point over filling, then roll wrapper over once. Moisten inside points with water. Bring side points together below filling, overlapping slightly; press together firmly to seal. Repeat with remaining wrappers and filling.* Keep finished wontons covered with plastic wrap while filling remaining wrappers.

3. Combine broth and remaining 1 tablespoon soy sauce in large saucepan. Bring to a boil over high heat. Reduce heat to medium; add wontons. Simmer 4 minutes or until filling is cooked through.

4. Stir in spinach, sliced pork, if desired, and green onions; remove from heat. Stir in sesame oil. Garnish each serving with shredded carrot.

*Makes 4 servings*

*\*Wontons may be made ahead to this point; cover and refrigerate up to 8 hours or freeze up to 3 months. Proceed as directed above if using refrigerated wontons; increase simmering time to 6 minutes if using frozen wontons.*

# spanish chicken and rice soup

**2 tablespoons vegetable oil**

**1 pound skinless, boneless chicken thighs, cut into cubes**

**1 large sweet onion, chopped (about 2 cups)**

**2 cloves garlic, minced**

**¼ teaspoon crushed red pepper**

**8 cups SWANSON® Chicken Broth (Regular, Natural Goodness® or Certified Organic)**

**1 can (14½ ounces) diced tomatoes, undrained**

**1 package (5 ounces) saffron yellow rice mix with seasoning**

**½ cup pitted green olives, sliced**

**¼ cup shredded fresh basil leaves**

1. Heat **1 tablespoon** of the oil in a 6-quart saucepot over medium-high heat. Add the chicken and cook until it's well browned, stirring often. Remove the chicken from the saucepot with a slotted spoon.

2. Add the remaining oil to the saucepot and reduce the heat to medium. Add the onion, garlic and red pepper and cook for 3 minutes.

3. Stir in the broth and tomatoes. Heat to a boil. Reduce the heat to low. Cover and cook for 15 minutes.

4. Stir in the rice and olives. Return the chicken to the saucepot. Cover and cook for 20 minutes or until the chicken is cooked through and the rice is done. Stir in the basil. Garnish with additional basil, if desired.

*Makes 6 servings*

Kitchen Tip: To shred fresh basil, select leaves that are not bruised or wilted. Stack the leaves and roll up. Slice with a sharp knife into very thin slices.

Prep Time: 15 minutes | Cook Time: 50 minutes

# short rib soup (kalbitang)

**2 pounds beef short ribs**

**2 quarts (8 cups) water**

**2 tablespoons dried cloud ear or other Oriental mushrooms**

**½ cup thinly sliced green onions**

**3 tablespoons soy sauce**

**2 tablespoons Sesame Salt (recipe follows)**

**1 tablespoon slivered garlic (about 2 cloves)**

**½ teaspoon dark sesame oil**

**¼ teaspoon red pepper flakes**

**1 egg, lightly beaten**

**1 bunch chives**

1. Score both sides of short ribs in diamond pattern with tip of sharp knife.

2. Bring ribs and water to a boil in Dutch oven or large saucepan over high heat. Reduce heat to low; cook, uncovered, about 1½ hours or until meat is tender. Remove ribs from broth. Skim fat from broth.

3. Meanwhile, place mushrooms in small bowl; cover with hot water. Let stand 30 minutes or until caps are soft. Drain; squeeze out excess water. Discard stems; slice caps.

4. Cut meat into bite-size pieces. Add beef, mushrooms, green onions, soy sauce, Sesame Salt, garlic, sesame oil and red pepper flakes to broth; cook 15 minutes over low heat.

5. Meanwhile, spray small omelet pan or skillet with nonstick cooking spray. Pour egg into pan; cook over medium-high heat until set on both sides. Cut omelet into strips. Garnish each serving with omelet strips and chives.

*Makes 4 servings*

Sesame Salt: Heat small skillet over medium heat. Add ½ cup sesame seeds; cook and stir about 3 minutes or until seeds are golden. Cool. Crush toasted sesame seeds and ¼ teaspoon salt with mortar and pestle or process in clean coffee or spice grinder. Store leftovers in refrigerator in covered glass jar.

# hot and sour soup

**1 package (1 ounce) dried shiitake mushrooms**
**4 cups chicken broth**
**3 tablespoons white vinegar**
**2 tablespoons soy sauce**
**½ to 1 teaspoon hot chili oil**
**¼ teaspoon white pepper**
**¼ pound firm tofu, patted dry and cut into ½-inch cubes**
**1 cup shredded cooked pork, chicken or turkey**
**½ cup drained canned bamboo shoots, cut into thin strips**
**3 tablespoons water**
**2 tablespoons cornstarch**
**1 egg white, lightly beaten**
**¼ cup thinly sliced green onions or chopped fresh cilantro**
**1 teaspoon dark sesame oil**

1. Place mushrooms in small bowl; cover with warm water. Let stand 20 minutes to soften. Drain; squeeze out excess water. Discard stems; slice caps.

2. Meanwhile, combine broth, vinegar, soy sauce, chili oil and white pepper in medium saucepan. Bring to a boil over high heat. Reduce heat to low; simmer 2 minutes.

3. Stir in mushrooms, tofu, pork and bamboo shoots; cook and stir until heated through.

4. Stir water into cornstarch in small bowl until smooth. Stir into soup until blended. Cook and stir 4 minutes or until soup boils and thickens. Remove from heat.

5. Stirring constantly in one direction, slowly pour egg white in thin stream into soup. Stir in green onions and sesame oil.

*Makes 4 to 6 servings*

# albondigas soup

1 pound ground beef

2 eggs, lightly beaten

¼ cup blue or yellow cornmeal

1 clove garlic, minced

1 tablespoon chopped fresh mint *or* 1 teaspoon crumbled dried mint

½ teaspoon salt

¼ teaspoon ground cumin

Dash black pepper

6 cups water

3 cans (10½ ounces each) condensed beef broth, undiluted

1 onion, chopped

¼ cup sliced celery

1 carrot, chopped

1 zucchini, chopped

1 yellow squash, chopped

½ bunch spinach, stemmed and cut into ½-inch strips

2 limes, cut into wedges

1. Combine beef, eggs, cornmeal, garlic, mint, salt, cumin and pepper in medium bowl. Shape mixture into 1-inch balls; set aside.

2. Combine water, broth, onion and celery in large saucepan or Dutch oven; bring to a boil over high heat. Reduce heat to low; simmer 10 minutes.

3. Add meatballs; simmer 5 minutes. Skim fat and foam from surface of broth. Add carrot, zucchini and yellow squash; simmer 20 minutes or until vegetables are tender.

4. Add spinach; simmer 5 minutes. Serve with lime wedges.

*Makes 6 servings*

# middle eastern chicken soup

**2½ cups water**
**1 can (about 14 ounces) reduced-sodium chicken broth**
**1 can (about 15 ounces) chickpeas, rinsed and drained**
**1 cup chopped cooked chicken**
**1 small onion, chopped**
**1 carrot, chopped**
**1 clove garlic, minced**
**1 teaspoon dried oregano**
**1 teaspoon ground cumin**
**½ (10-ounce) package fresh spinach, stemmed and coarsely chopped**
**⅛ teaspoon black pepper**

1. Combine water, broth, chickpeas, chicken, onion, carrot, garlic, oregano and cumin in medium saucepan. Bring to a boil over high heat. Reduce heat to low; cover and simmer 15 minutes.

2. Stir in spinach and pepper; simmer, uncovered, 2 minutes or until wilted.

*Makes 4 servings*

# mediterranean bean and sausage soup

**½ pound sweet or hot Italian pork sausage, casing removed**
**2 large onions, chopped (about 2 cups)**
**4 cups PREGO® Traditional Italian Sauce**
**2 cans (14 ounces each) SWANSON® Chicken Broth (Regular, Natural Goodness® or Certified Organic) (3½ cups)**
**2 cans (about 15 ounces each) black or pinto beans, rinsed and drained**
**2 cans (about 15 ounces each) white kidney (cannellini) beans or red kidney beans, rinsed and drained**

1. Cook the sausage and onions in a 3-quart saucepan over medium-high heat until the sausage is well browned, stirring frequently to break up meat. Pour off any fat.

2. Stir the sauce and broth into the saucepan. Heat to a boil. Reduce the heat to low. Cook for 10 minutes. Add the beans. Heat, stirring occasionally, until hot.

*Makes 8 servings*

Prep Time: 10 minutes │ Cook Time: 25 minutes

# spicy thai shrimp soup

1 tablespoon vegetable oil

1 pound medium raw shrimp, peeled, shells reserved

1 jalapeño pepper,* cut into slivers

1 tablespoon paprika

¼ teaspoon ground red pepper

4 cans (about 14 ounces each) reduced-sodium chicken broth

1 (½-inch) strip *each* lemon and lime peel

1 can (15 ounces) straw mushrooms, drained

Juice of 1 lemon

Juice of 1 lime

2 tablespoons reduced-sodium soy sauce

1 red Thai pepper,* red jalapeño pepper* *or* ¼ small red bell pepper, cut into strips

¼ cup fresh cilantro leaves

*Chile peppers can sting and irritate the skin, so wear rubber gloves when handling peppers and do not touch your eyes.*

1. Heat oil in large saucepan or wok over medium-high heat. Add shrimp, jalapeño, paprika and ground red pepper; cook and stir 2 minutes or until shrimp are pink and opaque. Remove from saucepan; set aside.

2. Add shrimp shells to saucepan; cook and stir 30 seconds. Add broth and lemon and lime peels; bring to a boil. Reduce heat to low; cover and simmer 15 minutes.

3. Remove shells and peels with slotted spoon; discard. Add mushrooms and shrimp mixture to broth; bring to a boil. Stir in lemon and lime juices, soy sauce and Thai pepper. Sprinkle each serving with cilantro. Serve immediately.

*Makes 8 servings*

# SLOW COOKER

## pumpkin soup with bacon and toasted pumpkin seeds

**2 teaspoons olive oil**

**½ cup raw pumpkin seeds**

**1 medium onion, chopped**

**1 teaspoon kosher salt**

**½ teaspoon chopped dried chipotle pepper**

**½ teaspoon black pepper**

**2 cans (29 ounces each) solid-pack pumpkin**

**4 cups chicken stock or broth**

**¾ cup apple cider**

**½ cup whipping cream**

**Sour cream**

**3 slices thick-sliced bacon, crisp-cooked and crumbled**

Slow Cooker Directions

1. Heat oil in medium skillet over medium heat. Add pumpkin seeds; cook and stir 1 minute or until seeds begin to pop. Transfer to small bowl; set aside.

2. Add onion to skillet; cook and stir over medium heat 5 minutes or until translucent. Stir in salt, chipotle pepper and black pepper. Transfer to slow cooker. Whisk in pumpkin, stock and apple cider; stir until smooth. Cover; cook on HIGH 4 hours.

3. Turn off slow cooker. Whisk in whipping cream. Season to taste with additional salt and pepper. Strain soup; garnish with sour cream, toasted pumpkin seeds and bacon.

*Makes 4 to 6 servings*

# moroccan chicken soup

**4 cups SWANSON® Chicken Broth (Regular, Natural Goodness® or Certified Organic)**

**3 cloves garlic, minced**

**2 tablespoons honey**

**2 teaspoons ground cumin**

**½ teaspoon ground cinnamon**

**1 can (about 14½ ounces) diced tomatoes, undrained**

**1 large green pepper, cut into 2-inch-long strips (about 2 cups)**

**1 medium onion, chopped (1 cup)**

**½ cup raisins**

**8 skinless, boneless chicken thighs (about 1 pound), cut up**

**Hot cooked orzo (optional)**

Slow Cooker Directions

1. Stir the broth, garlic, honey, cumin, cinnamon, tomatoes, green pepper, onion and raisins in a 3½- to 6-quart slow cooker. Add the chicken.

2. Cover and cook on LOW for 8 hours* or until the chicken is cooked through.

3. Divide the soup among **4** serving bowls. Place about ½ **cup** orzo centered on top of **each** of the serving bowls.

*Makes 4 servings*

*Or on HIGH for 4 hours*

Prep Time: 10 minutes │ Cook Time: 8 hours

# creamy cauliflower bisque

1 pound frozen cauliflower florets, thawed

1 pound russet potatoes, peeled and cut into 1-inch cubes

1 cup chopped onion

½ teaspoon dried thyme

¼ teaspoon garlic powder

⅛ teaspoon ground red pepper

2 cans (about 14 ounces each) reduced-sodium vegetable or chicken broth

1 cup evaporated milk

2 tablespoons butter

½ teaspoon salt

¼ teaspoon black pepper

1 cup (4 ounces) shredded sharp Cheddar cheese

¼ cup finely chopped fresh parsley

¼ cup finely chopped green onions

Slow Cooker Directions

1. Layer cauliflower, potatoes, onion, thyme, garlic powder and red pepper in slow cooker. Pour in broth. Cover; cook on LOW 8 hours or on HIGH 4 hours.

2. Process soup in batches in food processor or blender until smooth; return to slow cooker. Add evaporated milk, butter, salt and black pepper. Cook, uncovered, on HIGH 30 minutes or until heated through.

3. Top each serving with cheese, parsley and green onions.

*Makes 8 servings*

# nancy's chicken noodle soup

**2 boneless skinless chicken breasts, cut into bite-size pieces**

**⅔ cup diced onion**

**⅔ cup diced celery**

**⅔ cup diced carrots**

**⅔ cup sliced mushrooms**

**½ cup frozen peas**

**2 tablespoons butter or margarine**

**4 chicken bouillon cubes**

**1 tablespoon dried parsley flakes**

**1 teaspoon salt**

**1 teaspoon ground cumin**

**1 teaspoon dried marjoram**

**1 teaspoon black pepper**

**1 can (about 48 ounces) chicken broth**

**4 cups water**

**2 cups cooked egg noodles**

Slow Cooker Directions

1. Combine chicken, onion, celery, carrots, mushrooms, peas, butter, bouillon cubes, parsley flakes, salt, cumin, marjoram and pepper in slow cooker. Pour in broth and water.

2. Cover; cook on LOW 5 to 7 hours or on HIGH 3 to 4 hours. Stir in noodles 30 minutes before serving.

*Makes 8 servings*

# potato & spinach soup with gouda

**6 cups cubed peeled Yukon Gold potatoes (about 9 medium)**
**2 cans (about 14 ounces each) vegetable or chicken broth**
**½ cup water**
**1 small red onion, finely chopped**
**5 ounces baby spinach**
**½ teaspoon salt**
**¼ teaspoon ground red pepper**
**¼ teaspoon black pepper**
**2½ cups shredded smoked Gouda cheese, divided**
**1 can (12 ounces) evaporated milk**
**1 tablespoon olive oil**
**4 cloves garlic, cut into thin slices**
**Chopped fresh parsley**

Slow Cooker Directions

1. Combine potatoes, broth, water, onion, spinach, salt, red pepper and black pepper in slow cooker. Cover; cook on LOW 10 hours or on HIGH 4 to 5 hours.

2. *Turn slow cooker to HIGH.* Slightly mash potatoes in slow cooker; add 2 cups cheese and evaporated milk. Cover; cook on HIGH 15 to 20 minutes or until cheese is melted.

3. Heat oil in small skillet over low heat. Add garlic; cook and stir 2 minutes or until golden brown. Sprinkle soup with garlic, remaining ½ cup cheese and parsley.

*Makes 8 to 10 servings*

Tip: Yukon Gold potatoes are thin-skinned, pale yellow-gold potatoes with pale yellow flesh. When buying potatoes, make sure there are no bruises, sprouts or green areas. Store Yukon Golds in a cool dark place and use within 1 week of purchase.

# hearty mushroom and barley soup

9 cups vegetable or chicken broth

1 package (16 ounces) sliced button mushrooms

1 onion, chopped

2 carrots, chopped

2 stalks celery, chopped

½ cup uncooked pearl barley

½ ounce dried porcini mushrooms

3 cloves garlic, minced

1 teaspoon salt

½ teaspoon dried thyme

½ teaspoon black pepper

Slow Cooker Directions

Combine broth, button mushrooms, onion, carrots, celery, barley, porcini mushrooms, garlic, salt, thyme and pepper in slow cooker. Cover; cook on LOW 4 to 6 hours.

*Makes 8 to 10 servings*

Variation: For even more flavor, add a beef or ham bone to the slow cooker with the rest of the ingredients.

# navy bean and ham soup

6 cups water

5 cups dried navy beans, soaked overnight, rinsed and drained

1 pound ham, cubed

1 can (about 15 ounces) whole kernel corn, drained

1 can (4 ounces) mild diced green chiles, drained

1 onion, diced

Salt and black pepper

Slow Cooker Directions

Combine water, beans, ham, corn, chiles, onion, salt and pepper in slow cooker. Cover; cook on LOW 8 to 10 hours or until beans are softened.

*Makes 6 servings*

# classic french onion soup

¼ cup (½ stick) butter

3 large onions, sliced

1 cup dry white wine

3 cans (about 14 ounces each) beef or vegetable broth

1 teaspoon Worcestershire sauce

½ teaspoon salt

½ teaspoon dried thyme

4 slices French bread, toasted

1 cup (4 ounces) shredded Swiss cheese

Slow Cooker Directions

1. Melt butter in large skillet over medium heat. Add onions; cook and stir 15 minutes or until onions are soft and lightly browned. Stir in wine.

2. Combine onion mixture, broth, Worcestershire sauce, salt and thyme in slow cooker. Cover; cook on LOW 4 to 4½ hours.

3. Preheat broiler. Ladle soup into 4 ovenproof bowls; top with bread slice and cheese. Broil until cheese melts.

*Makes 4 servings*

# slow cooker sausage vegetable soup

1 pound BOB EVANS® Original Recipe Sausage Roll

3 cans (14 ounces each) reduced sodium chicken broth

1 package (20 ounces) BOB EVANS® Home Fries diced potatoes

1 package (16 ounces) frozen mixed vegetables

1 can (8 ounces) tomato sauce

Slow Cooker Directions

In a medium skillet over medium heat, crumble and cook sausage until brown. Place in slow cooker. Add remaining ingredients. Cover and cook on LOW 6 to 8 hours.

*Makes 8 servings*

Prep Time: **10 minutes** | Cook Time: 6 to 8 hours

# sweet and sour cabbage soup

    2 pounds boneless beef chuck roast
    1 can (about 28 ounces) whole tomatoes, cut into pieces, undrained
    1 can (15 ounces) tomato sauce
    1 large onion, thinly sliced
    3 carrots, shredded
    2 pounds green cabbage, shredded
    4 cups water
    ¾ cup sugar
    ½ cup lemon juice
    1 tablespoon caraway seeds
    2 teaspoons salt
    1 teaspoon black pepper

Slow Cooker Directions

1. Cut beef into 4 pieces. Spray large skillet with nonstick cooking spray; heat over medium-high heat. Brown meat on all sides; transfer to slow cooker. Add tomatoes, tomato sauce, onion, carrots, cabbage, water, sugar, lemon juice, caraway seeds, salt and pepper. Cover; cook on LOW 6 to 8 hours.

2. Remove beef from slow cooker. Shred beef and return to slow cooker; heat through.

*Makes 8 to 10 servings*

# thai coconut chicken and rice soup

**1 pound boneless skinless chicken thighs, cut into 1-inch pieces**

**3 cups reduced-sodium chicken broth**

**1 package (12 ounces) frozen chopped onions**

**1 can (4 ounces) sliced mushrooms, drained**

**2 tablespoons minced fresh ginger**

**2 tablespoons sugar**

**1 can (14 ounces) unsweetened coconut milk**

**1 cup cooked rice**

**½ red bell pepper, seeded and thinly sliced**

**3 tablespoons chopped fresh cilantro**

**2 tablespoons grated lime peel**

Slow Cooker Directions

1. Combine chicken, broth, onions, mushrooms, ginger and sugar in slow cooker. Cover; cook on LOW 8 to 9 hours.

2. Stir coconut milk, rice and bell pepper into soup. Cover; cook 15 minutes. Turn off heat; stir in cilantro and lime peel.

*Makes 6 to 8 servings*

Tip: One medium lime will yield about 1½ teaspoons grated lime peel. You will need about 4 medium limes to get 2 tablespoons grated lime peel.

# italian sausage soup

### Meatballs

**1 pound mild Italian sausage, casings removed**

**½ cup plain dry bread crumbs**

**¼ cup grated Parmesan cheese**

**¼ cup milk**

**1 egg**

**½ teaspoon dried basil**

**½ teaspoon black pepper**

**¼ teaspoon garlic salt**

### Soup

**4 cups chicken broth**

**1 tablespoon tomato paste**

**1 clove garlic, minced**

**¼ teaspoon red pepper flakes**

**½ cup uncooked miniature shell pasta***

**1 package (10 ounces) baby spinach**

**Additional grated Parmesan cheese (optional)**

*Or use other tiny pasta, such as ditalini (mini tubes) or farfallini (mini bowties).*

### Slow Cooker Directions

1. Combine all meatball ingredients in large bowl. Shape into ½-inch balls.

2. Combine broth, tomato paste, garlic and red pepper flakes in slow cooker. Add meatballs. Cover; cook on LOW 5 to 6 hours.

3. Add pasta; cook 30 minutes or until pasta is tender. Stir in spinach. Sprinkle with additional cheese, if desired. Serve immediately.

*Makes 4 to 6 servings*

# slow-simmered chicken rice soup

½ **cup uncooked wild rice**

½ **cup uncooked regular long-grain white rice**

1 **tablespoon vegetable oil**

5¼ **cups SWANSON® Chicken Broth (Regular, Natural Goodness® or Certified Organic)**

2 **teaspoons dried thyme leaves, crushed**

¼ **teaspoon crushed red pepper**

2 **stalks celery, coarsely chopped (about 1 cup)**

1 **medium onion, chopped (about ½ cup)**

1 **pound skinless, boneless chicken breasts, cut into cubes**

**Sour cream (optional)**

**Chopped green onions (optional)**

Slow Cooker Directions

1. Stir the wild rice, white rice and oil in a 3½-quart slow cooker. Cover and cook on HIGH for 15 minutes.

2. Stir the broth, thyme, red pepper, celery, onion and chicken into the slow cooker. Turn the heat to LOW. Cover and cook on LOW for 7 to 8 hours* or until the chicken is cooked through.

3. Serve with the sour cream and green onions, if desired.

*Makes 8 servings*

*Or on HIGH for 4 to 5 hours

Time-Saving Tip: Speed preparation by substituting 3 cans (4.5 ounces each) SWANSON® Premium Chunk Chicken Breast, drained, for the raw chicken.

Prep Time: 15 minutes │ Cook Time: 7 to 8 hours (LOW) • 4 to 5 hours (HIGH)

# double corn chowder

**1 cup corn**
**1 cup canned hominy**
**6 ounces Canadian bacon, chopped**
**2 stalks celery, chopped**
**1 small onion or large shallot, chopped**
**1 jalapeño pepper,\* seeded and minced**
**¼ teaspoon salt**
**¼ teaspoon dried thyme**
**¼ teaspoon black pepper**
**1 cup chicken broth**
**1½ cups milk,\*\* divided**
**1 tablespoon all-purpose flour**

*\*Jalapeño peppers can sting and irritate the skin, so wear rubber gloves when handling peppers and do not touch your eyes.*

*\*\*For richer chowder, use ¾ cup milk and ¾ cup half-and-half.*

Slow Cooker Directions

1. Combine corn, hominy, bacon, celery, onion, jalapeño, salt, thyme and black pepper in slow cooker. Add broth. Cover; cook on LOW 5 to 6 hours or on HIGH 3 to 3½ hours.

2. Whisk 2 tablespoons milk into flour in small bowl until smooth. Stir into slow cooker. Add remaining milk. Cover; cook on LOW 20 minutes or until slightly thickened and heated through.

*Makes 4 servings*

# tuscan white bean soup

  6 ounces bacon, diced
10 cups chicken broth
  1 package (16 ounces) dried Great Northern beans, rinsed and sorted
  1 can (about 14 ounces) diced tomatoes
  1 large onion, chopped
  3 carrots, chopped
  4 cloves garlic, minced
  1 fresh rosemary sprig *or* 1 teaspoon dried rosemary
  1 teaspoon black pepper

Slow Cooker Directions

1. Cook bacon in medium skillet over medium heat until crisp; drain on paper towels. Transfer to slow cooker. Add broth, beans, tomatoes, onion, carrots, garlic, rosemary and pepper.

2. Cover; cook on LOW 8 hours or until beans are tender. Remove and discard rosemary before serving.

*Makes 8 to 10 servings*

Serving Suggestion: Place slices of toasted Italian bread in bottom of individual soup bowls. Drizzle with olive oil. Ladle soup over bread.

# butternut squash-apple soup

3 packages (12 ounces each) frozen cooked winter squash, thawed and drained *or* about 4½ cups mashed cooked butternut squash
2 cans (about 14 ounces each) vegetable broth
1 medium Golden Delicious apple, peeled and chopped
2 tablespoons minced onion
1 tablespoon packed brown sugar
1 teaspoon minced fresh sage *or* ½ teaspoon ground sage
¼ teaspoon ground ginger
½ cup whipping cream or half-and-half

Slow Cooker Directions

1. Combine squash, broth, apple, onion, brown sugar, sage and ginger in slow cooker.

2. Cover; cook on LOW 6 hours or on HIGH 3 hours.

3. Process soup in batches in food processor or blender until smooth. Return to slow cooker. Stir in cream just before serving.

*Makes 6 to 8 servings*

tuscan white bean soup

# roasted tomato-basil soup

**2 cans (28 ounces each) whole tomatoes, drained and juice reserved**
**1 onion, finely chopped**
**2½ tablespoons packed dark brown sugar**
**3 cups vegetable or chicken broth**
**3 tablespoons tomato paste**
**¼ teaspoon ground allspice**
**1 can (5 ounces) evaporated milk**
**¼ cup chopped fresh basil**
**Salt and black pepper**
**Additional fresh basil (optional)**

Slow Cooker Directions

1. Preheat oven to 450°F. Line baking sheet with foil; spray with nonstick cooking spray. Arrange tomatoes on foil in single layer. Sprinkle with onion and brown sugar. Bake 25 to 30 minutes or until tomatoes look dry and are lightly browned. Let tomatoes cool slightly; finely chop.

2. Place tomato mixture, reserved tomato juice, broth, tomato paste and allspice in slow cooker; mix well. Cover; cook on LOW 8 hours or on HIGH 4 hours.

3. Add evaporated milk and basil; season with salt and pepper. Cook on HIGH 30 minutes or until heated through. Garnish with fresh basil.

*Makes 6 servings*

# ACKNOWLEDGMENTS

The publisher would like to thank the companies and organizations listed below for the use of their recipes and photographs in this publication.

Bob Evans®

Campbell Soup Company

ConAgra Foods, Inc.

Del Monte Foods

Dole Food Company, Inc.

Filippo Berio® Olive Oil

Jennie-O Turkey Store, LLC

McIlhenny Company (TABASCO® brand Pepper Sauce)

Michael Foods, Inc.

National Fisheries Institute

National Pork Board

Ortega®, A Division of B&G Foods, Inc.

Reckitt Benckiser Inc.

StarKist®

Unilever

# METRIC CONVERSION CHART

## VOLUME MEASUREMENTS (dry)

$\frac{1}{8}$ teaspoon = 0.5 mL
$\frac{1}{4}$ teaspoon = 1 mL
$\frac{1}{2}$ teaspoon = 2 mL
$\frac{3}{4}$ teaspoon = 4 mL
1 teaspoon = 5 mL
1 tablespoon = 15 mL
2 tablespoons = 30 mL
$\frac{1}{4}$ cup = 60 mL
$\frac{1}{3}$ cup = 75 mL
$\frac{1}{2}$ cup = 125 mL
$\frac{2}{3}$ cup = 150 mL
$\frac{3}{4}$ cup = 175 mL
1 cup = 250 mL
2 cups = 1 pint = 500 mL
3 cups = 750 mL
4 cups = 1 quart = 1 L

## VOLUME MEASUREMENTS (fluid)

1 fluid ounce (2 tablespoons) = 30 mL
4 fluid ounces ($\frac{1}{2}$ cup) = 125 mL
8 fluid ounces (1 cup) = 250 mL
12 fluid ounces (1$\frac{1}{2}$ cups) = 375 mL
16 fluid ounces (2 cups) = 500 mL

## WEIGHTS (mass)

$\frac{1}{2}$ ounce = 15 g
1 ounce = 30 g
3 ounces = 90 g
4 ounces = 120 g
8 ounces = 225 g
10 ounces = 285 g
12 ounces = 360 g
16 ounces = 1 pound = 450 g

## DIMENSIONS

$\frac{1}{16}$ inch = 2 mm
$\frac{1}{8}$ inch = 3 mm
$\frac{1}{4}$ inch = 6 mm
$\frac{1}{2}$ inch = 1.5 cm
$\frac{3}{4}$ inch = 2 cm
1 inch = 2.5 cm

## OVEN TEMPERATURES

250°F = 120°C
275°F = 140°C
300°F = 150°C
325°F = 160°C
350°F = 180°C
375°F = 190°C
400°F = 200°C
425°F = 220°C
450°F = 230°C

## BAKING PAN SIZES

| Utensil | Size in Inches/Quarts | Metric Volume | Size in Centimeters |
|---|---|---|---|
| Baking or Cake Pan (square or rectangular) | 8×8×2 | 2 L | 20×20×5 |
| | 9×9×2 | 2.5 L | 23×23×5 |
| | 12×8×2 | 3 L | 30×20×5 |
| | 13×9×2 | 3.5 L | 33×23×5 |
| Loaf Pan | 8×4×3 | 1.5 L | 20×10×7 |
| | 9×5×3 | 2 L | 23×13×7 |
| Round Layer Cake Pan | 8×1½ | 1.2 L | 20×4 |
| | 9×1½ | 1.5 L | 23×4 |
| Pie Plate | 8×1¼ | 750 mL | 20×3 |
| | 9×1¼ | 1 L | 23×3 |
| Baking Dish or Casserole | 1 quart | 1 L | — |
| | 1½ quart | 1.5 L | — |
| | 2 quart | 2 L | — |